Getting Your Act Together

Four plays to help teens choose the right roles in life

by Theresa Hayes

Cover illustration by Kay Salem

STANDARD PUBLISHING
Cincinnati, Ohio   3358

Library of Congress Cataloging-in-Publication Data

Hayes, Theresa.
  Getting your act together.

  Summary: Four plays with a religious emphasis help young teens identify proper and improper behavior, dealing with manners, honesty, modesty, and family relationships.
  1. Young adult drama, American. 2. Didactic drama, American. 3. Christian drama, American. [1. Behavior—Drama. 2. Christian life—Drama. 3. Plays] I. Title.
  PS3558.A838G48   1986   812'.54   85-16548
  ISBN 0-87239-998-2

Copyright © 1986, The STANDARD PUBLISHING Company, Cincinnati, Ohio, Division of STANDEX INTERNATIONAL Corporation. Printed in U.S.A.

Scripture quotes in this book are from the *Holy Bible: New International Version,* © 1973, 1978, International Bible Society. Used by permission of Zondervan Bible Publishers and the International Bible Society.

ABOUT THIS BOOK....

There are four, full-length (sixty to ninety minutes), modern-day plays for teenagers in this book. Teens can play the roles of adults in any or all of the plays, but you'll need two particularly good actors or actresses to play the two leading adult characters in "Fractured Families." Also, a mayor and a high-school principal have fairly lengthy speeches in "Like a Careless Match." Adult players might lend realism to your production, but an all-teen cast will give teens the opportunity to see life from their parents' point of view.

The lead in "Like a Careless Match" is written for a boy, but there is no reason why you couldn't make it a girl's part. Simply change the character's name and a few lines of dialogue when necessary. Allow flexibility in the casting of all the plays to take best advantage of the acting talent available to you.

"Fractured Families" and "Manners Matter" each contain twenty pages of dialogue, which should equal between forty-five and sixty minutes of stage time. "Gentlemen Prefer Ladies" has twenty-five pages, and "Like a Careless Match" has twenty-seven pages of dialogue. Add time to arrange sets between acts, and time for a short intermission, and allow between an hour and an hour and a half for each presentation.

No special costumes are required for any play, and only a few props will be needed for "Like a Careless Match." Scenes take place in homes, schools, and churches, with one scene in McDonald's. If you print a program identifying the location of each scene, you can get by with a minimum of scenery.

The discussion questions at the end of each play are designed to take your teens beyond the action of the characters into the analysis of their motivation—and possibly into a better understanding of their own behavior. To be most effective, your teens should not see the questions, or even know that they exist, until you are ready for the discussion. Allow them to "get into" the characters without worrying about having to explain their behavior later.

As a youth worker, you probably already know that anything you do with your teens—any time you spend together—allows you to know each other better and grow closer together. Producing a play will give you a *lot* of time together! Don't spread your rehearsals over such a long period of time that you all grow sick of the play, but do be sure to allow ample time to learn the lines, rehearse the stage movements, and have *at least* one, complete dress rehearsal. Juggle and publish your rehearsal times by scenes, so that only the persons in scene two (for example) need to be present at 7:00, to be joined by the persons in scene three at 7:30, and joined by the entire cast (perhaps) at 8:00.

After you and your teens have spent so many hours in preparation, why not take your presentation to a neighboring church, teen rally, or area overnighter? Have an ample supply of the discussion questions to distribute then, to get the reactions of teens who are seeing the material for the first time.

How will you get these multiple copies? As you know, most printed matter is copyrighted to protect the publisher and author from loss of sales. This book is no exception, but "Like a Careless Match" has thirty speaking parts (some only one or two lines long), and we wouldn't want you to have to buy that many copies of the book. Therefore, we are hereby giving special permission to copy the plays and discussion question in this book. For one church to buy a copy of the book and provide another church with copies of a script, or to loan the book for that purpose, would of course be an abuse of this special permission. We trust our buyers to act accordingly.

The pages of this book are perforated to allow easy removal and distribution of the scripts and discussion questions.

Even if you don't put on a full—blown production, but read the plays aloud in groups, my fondest hope is that these plays will help teens make wise decisions concerning the roles they want to play in life. With all the compelling influences of the world today, the choices have never been more difficult, nor more necessary.

—*Theresa Hayes*

CONTENTS

Manners Matter   7
When rude behavior disrupts a worship service, six teens are held responsible. Later, two of them receive an unforgettable lesson in the importance of courtesy.

Fractured Families   31
Two guest lecturers teach keys to communication to high-school students and their parents, and get them to share the single biggest deterrent to teenage suicide—love.

Gentlemen Prefer Ladies (and vice versa)   55
The rape of a local high-school girl incites an emotional youth-group discussion on the need for modesty in today's world.

Like a Careless Match   83
A single, jealous remark grows into a citywide scandal, destroying friendships, families, and reputations, until the guilty teen confesses.

MANNERS MATTER

CAST OF CHARACTERS
Julie
Karen
Beth
Brian
Matt
Steve
(All of the above are high-school students in the same grade.)
Mr. Miller—leads worship service at church Usher
Mr. Jones, Mr. Taylor, Mr. Wells—deacons or elders
Josh, Todd, Erica, LeeAnn—schoolmates
Beth's mom
Steve's dad
Adult and teen extras

SCENES
Act 1 Scene 1: Church auditorium
Act 1 Scene 2: Sunday-school room
Act 2 Scene 1: Beth's and Steve's bedrooms
Act 2 Scene 2: School cafeteria
Act 2 Scenes 3 and 4: Beth's and Steve's bedrooms

ACT 1, SCENE 1

The stage is set up to look like the auditorium of a church building. There are several rows of chairs (pews) sitting at an angle from the back of the stage to the front, with an aisle down the middle. The *back* of the pulpit will be facing the audience in the center, or catercornered off to one side of the stage (see illustration).

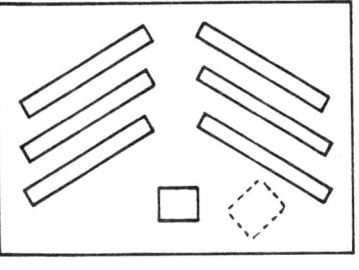

Julie, Karen, Beth, and Brian are entering the sanctuary just as the service is beginning. An usher leads them to a space between adults just big enough for four and leaves. Just then, two other boys rush up the aisle to join them. When they are all seated, they should be in this order: Beth, Brian, Julie, Karen, Matt, and Steve.

7

Matt *(whispering loudly):* Hey you guys! Is there room for us?
Steve: Move over! Hurry! Church is about to start!
(Adults move closer together and closer to the aisles and the kids scrunch up to make room as the two latecomers climb clumsily over the adults. As Steve squeezes into the last space, he knocks the lady's hymnbook onto the floor.)
Steve *(as the others are laughing and giggling):* Ooops! 'Scuse me.
(Lady frowns at him, waits a minute, obviously expecting him to pick up the book, then leans over to pick it up herself.)
Worship Leader *(from the front):* Welcome to the Lord's house this beautiful morning! Let us begin to prepare our hearts to worship Him by singing verses one and three of hymn number 111, "O Worship the King."
(Kids are squirming, punching, giggling, flipping pages in the hymnals during this announcement.)
Julie: What page did he say?
Brian: *I donno. I didn't hear it either.*
(An adult sitting in front of them turns around and shows his open hymnal, and points to the page number.)
Julie *(in a loud whisper):* Oh! Thank you!
Brian *(to other kids):* Page 111!
Karen *(shuffling her book):* OK!
Beth: I already have it—see? *(Shows her book to them.)*
Matt: Is that 111 or 211?
Congregation starts to sing, "O worship the King, all glorious above ..."
(As the singing continues softly, Brian leans past Karen and Julie to speak to Steve and Matt.)
Brian: Hey! I saw you guys at Cinema 5 last night—what did you see?
Matt: "Revenge of the Blood Suckers"—what did you see?
Steve *(interrupting before Matt can answer):* Oh man! It was neat! I never saw so much blood in all my life!
(Karen and Julie have continued to sing, while trying to listen to the boys at the same time. Now, however ...)
Julie *(drops her book loudly onto the top of the pew in front of her and says loudly):* Oh gross!
(Adults around them have been frowning at the conversation during the singing. When the book drops, they all jump and turn to glare.)
Julie *(covers mouth):* Ooops!
(Kids join in singing for a phrase or two, then ...)
Matt *(whispers to Brian):* So what movie did you see?

8

(Before he can answer, Karen begins to flirt with him.)
Karen: And who were you *with,* huh Brian?
Brian *(in a disgusted tone, to Matt):* I saw "Star Wrecker!" *(Turns to Karen):* And I was *with* my brother!
(Brian lifts his hymnal and begins singing loudly as Julie punches Karen and both girls giggle.)
Julie: Honestly Karen! You don't have to be so obvious!
Karen: What's so obvious? I just asked him who he was with!
(Both girls giggle again and an adult behind them whispers a loud, "Shhhh!" The kids settle down and finish singing the hymn.)
Worship Leader: Let us continue to worship the Lord, now in prayer. *(The congregation bows their heads.)* Our dear heavenly Father, we come before you this morning asking that You would humble us—give us the hearts and minds of loving, grateful servants, so that we might come before You with the proper attitude and spirit. *(He continues to pray throughout the following exchange.)*
Steve *(leans over and whispers to Brian—who is on the other end of the row):* Psst! Hey Brian!
(Several adults are startled into a jump, and a jerk of the head, one man turns and frowns at Steve. Brian continues to leave his head bowed, eyes closed. Julie and Karen look up at Steve when he begins to speak, then turn their heads toward Brian for his response. Now they turn back to Steve again ...)
Steve: Hey, Brian!
(This time, Matt and Beth lift their heads and join Julie and Karen first in looking at Steve, then Brian, all in unison, tennis match style.)
Brian *(slowly turns his head sideways and opens one eye to look at Steve):* Quiet, Man! Can't you see that I'm praying? *(He lowers his head again as all four of the others turn towards Steve.)*
Steve: Well excuuuse me! *(To others):* When did he get so religious?
(Matt, Karen, Julie, and Beth all snicker and poke each other during this exchange.)
Karen *(leans over Matt to speak to Steve in a sympathetic tone of voice):* His old man comes down on him pretty hard. I think he's probably afraid of him.
(Steve looks surprised, Matt nods in agreement.)
Worship Leader: We pray these things in Jesus' name, amen.
(Everyone sits down as the organ begins to softly play Brahmns' "Lullaby." At the first notes, Karen slaps her hand over her mouth and then begins sniffing loudly. The following

dialogue takes place simultaneously.)

Julie *(groans)*: Oh no!
Matt: What's the matter with her?
Beth: She get this way *every time* they announce that a new baby has been born! She's such a crybaby!
Karen: I am not! I just can't help but cry when I hear that song! And then when the parents carry that little, tiny baby down the aisle— oh look! Here they come now!

Worship Leader: As you know, the rosebud on the pulpit signifies the birth of a new little one in our midst. Jim and Kathy Anderson proudly announce the arrival of their first daughter, Jennifer Elaine. We now invite Miss Jennifer Elaine Anderson to bring her parents to the front of the sanctuary so that we might pray for her and for her family.

(As everyone turns to look, Karen weeps loudly while several others in the congregation ooh and ahh. As the family passes, a man in the pew in front of the kids steps out into the aisle and leaves.)

Julie: Where's he going?
Beth: Well where do you think, dummy? Probably to the "little boys' room."

(The boys react with exaggerated embarrassment and the girls break up in laughter, as if this were the funniest thing they've ever heard. By this time, the Anderson family has made it to the front and the worship leader was just beginning to pray for them. When the girls break out laughing, he is so startled that he loses his place. This causes all six kids to laugh again.)

Brian *(still laughing)*: Cut it out, you guys! We're gonna get in trouble!

(Just then, the man who had been sitting in front of the kids returns with an elder and points to the kids. As the entire congregation waits and watches, the elder leans over and speaks to them.)

Elder: Will all of you kids please come with me?

(They all look surprised. Then Steve and Beth feign innocence, Matt and Julie look embarrassed, and Karen and Brian looks scared.)

Steve: What for?
Julie: I can't believe this is happening.
Brian: My dad's going to kill me!
Elder: Come along now, don't make me wait all day—you're holding up the service.

(The kids glance at the people around them, who are all watching,

and at the worship leader, who is indeed waiting for them to leave. They begin to get up and the couple on the end of the aisle steps out to let them pass.)

Julie (quietly): I am *soooo* embarrassed!

Karen: Sshhh! Everybody's watching!

Brian (shaking his head sadly): I'm gonna be dead meat! *(They all shuffle out, heads hanging, the couple returns to their seats, and the worship leader begins praying.)*

Worship Leader: Father, we are joined now in asking for your guidance as Jim and Kathy attempt to rear this child to be a follower of You.

END OF SCENE 1

ACT 1, SCENE 2

The first elder has been joined by two others and they are with the six kids in a Sunday-school room. The kids are sitting in a row in the middle of the room, with empty chairs all around them. One elder has turned a chair around backwards and is sitting on it, facing them, resting his arms on the back of the chair, a second is sitting on the edge of a desk, swinging his leg, and the third elder is pacing the room.

Mr. Jones: *(sitting on desk):* Well, you kids have finally managed to disrupt the entire worship service and bring it to a screeching halt. I was afraid this would happen sooner or later.

Mr. Taylor: *(sitting on chair):* I just don't understand this type of behavior at all—I knew you all in junior church, and you were such a *nice* bunch of kids then—what happened?

Mr. Wells *(pacing):* And you're all from good families! It's not as if you haven't been taught better *manners.* Why, Brian, your father is chairman of the elders, what do you think he is going to say about this situation?

Brian *(putting his head in his hands):* I'm gonna be dead meat when I get home.

Jones: What? Speak up, I can't hear you!

Brian *(snapping his head to attention):* I said, he isn't going to like it at all, Sir.

Steve *(defiantly):* Oh good grief! What's this "sir" business? I don't see what the big deal is—so we were making a little noise ...

(The three elders interrupt and speak in rapid order.)

Jones: "Sir" is Brian's attempt to show some measure of respect—an example that you could learn from!

Taylor: The "big deal" is that you interrupted everyone within hearing range of you—people who were trying to worship God! What makes you think your chatter is more important than that?

Wells: And I'd hardly call it "a little noise" when you interrupted Mr. Miller, clear up in the front of the sanctuary! And besides, this is not the first time someone has complained to us about your poor *manners!*

Beth: What do you keep talking about manners for? I've got good manners! What has that got to do with this?

Wells: You *have* good manners? Well, where do you keep them?

Taylor *(to Wells):* Now John ... *(to kids):* What do you think manners are? *(Silence.)*

Taylor: Please, I'm serious. I'd like to hear your definition of good manners. Steve? Beth? Brian?

Brian: Well, a guy with good manners opens doors for ladies.

Karen: And my mom always makes me write thank-you notes because she says people will think I'm bad mannered if I don't.

Julie: Yeah, and my mom says it's bad manners to talk with your mouth full.

Taylor *(sighs):* Yes, but what do those actions signify?

Kids *(in unison):* Huh?

Taylor: What do opening doors for others, writing thank-you notes—or simply saying "please" and "thank you"—and not talking with food in your mouth have in common?

Matt: Well, they're all ways to act polite. ...

Karen: They're ways to be courteous ... to show respect.

Wells: Exactly! Respect for another person's rights or feelings!

Steve: But that doesn't explain why we're supposed to "respect" everyone around us! What about *our* rights and freedoms?

Beth: Yeah! You can't force us to be quiet and listen, you know! *(The three men shake their heads sadly. Steve and Beth maintain a defiant, rebellious attitude, Julie and Matt are now a little embarrassed by Steve and Beth, while Brian and Karen look absolutely miserable.)*

Karen: Look Beth, I don't think they're talking about *forcing* us to do anything. I mean, if we *have* good manners....

Matt: Well, who can learn all those stupid rules and remember 'em all? Personally, I think it's real dumb to have to learn which fork to use and when to put your napkin on your lap! *(The other kids all nod and agree.)*

Jones: We're not talking about rules of etiquette here—although they are just an elaborate way of expressing courtesy—we're talking about basic manners that enable us to get along together in this world. We'd be in an awful mess without manners!

Wells: *And,* we're talking about a manner of respect that ought to be shown *here,* in God's house, especially!

Jones: *Not only* a respect for those around you who are trying to worship, but a respect for God himself. It *is* conversation with Him that you are interrupting.

Taylor: One would have to be pretty rude and arrogant to think that whatever he or she had to say was more important than the prayers and praise being offered to God.

Jones: And you should know that most of the songs we sing are praises to God.

Wells: Or, the words to the hymn might be words of prayer, asking God for strength or guidance.

Jones: Or, as was the case this morning, the words to "O Worship the King" were written to inspire us to develop an attitude of reverence toward God—"to prepare our hearts for worship," as Mr. Miller said.

Wells: And even if *you* don't feel worshipful, or reverent, or even care that you are in the house of God, you still have no right to force your disrespectful attitude on people around you.

Beth: Why don't we?

Jones: Someone once said, "My rights end where the other guy's rights begin."

Steve: What's that supposed to mean?

Wells: It *means* that your right to talk freely with your friends ends when the people around you have the right to expect silence from you.

Jones: Whether that be in church, or in a movie theater, or at a concert—or even in school!

Taylor: The funny thing about that is that people will often show more respect for the strangers in a movie theater than they will for fellow worshipers in the house of God. Maybe that's because we don't expect people in church to turn around and tell us to "shut up" like a stranger might do at a show. But why respond to the kindness and freedom we find in the church building by being rude?

Wells: Which brings up another point about rudeness. So far we've talked about showing respect for God, and for the people sitting around us, but how do you think Mr. Miller felt—and the young Anderson family—when you kids were cutting up during their presentation?

Karen *(after a short pause):* I guess if I was a new mother introducing my brand-new baby, I'd feel pretty bad if people didn't even care enough to be quiet.

Taylor: Karen, you've hit the nail on the head. There may be many people in our congregation who don't care a thing about meeting the new babies, but they can put themselves in the young parents' place enough to realize how important this is for them—and that's really all that good manners are—putting yourself in another person's place and imagining what would make them feel better, or make their job easier for them.

Wells: And having led the service myself, I can tell you that it is hard to try and keep things moving along, in order, and to remember everything I'm supposed to say, and to try to help people develop an attitude of worship. Having a bunch of kids creating a disturbance is *not* appreciated!

(The kids are all looking pretty shame-faced after this lecture. After an embarrassed silence....)

Brian: You know, hearing you say that really makes me feel ashamed. I *know* you, Mr. Wells, you've been to our house for dinner. I guess if I thought of the man up in the pulpit as a person with feelings instead of just some guy, maybe I wouldn't be so rude.

Karen: I guess I never thought of it like that either.

Matt: Me neither. But Mr. Jones, what did you mean about manners making us get along together? I don't get it.

Jones *(patiently):* Good manners are nothing more than being aware of another person's situation and feelings. We write thank-you notes not only to express our gratitude, but also so that the person who did something nice for us will *know* that we appreciate it—they won't have to wonder, or imagine that they did or sent the wrong thing, or think that the gift got lost in the mail.

Taylor: And we don't talk with food in our mouths because that is disgusting to the person who is watching us. It's the same reason we cover our mouths when we cough, and don't pick our noses!

Julie: Oh gross!

Taylor: Exactly. And because we don't want people to think we are gross, we try not to be.

Karen: Sometimes the boys—well, all of us, really—try to be gross on purpose.

Wells: *That* is part of adolescence! Hopefully you will outgrow that, someday!

Jones: I believe you all are starting to get the picture, but, the fact remains that you have to be disciplined. This situation has been discussed at our elders meeting and we've decided that you won't be allowed to sit together until you've demonstrated that you've learned how to behave in church.

Taylor: The three of us, and all the other elders, will be looking for you at the start of each service—

Jones: and if you're sitting together, we'll come and separate you—

Wells: or, we may just sit down between you!

Beth *(shoots up out of her chair and shouts at the elders):* You're treating us like babies!

Wells: I'm afraid you asked for it, my dear! *(Beth slumps angrily back into her chair.)*

Jones: As I said, when you've demonstrated that you can act in a mature, courteous manner, we'll allow you to sit by yourselves. In the meantime, we have a responsibility to the rest of the congregation, so if you don't want to be publicly embarrassed each Sunday, please comply with this request.

Brian: Is that all? I mean, are you going to tell our parents, or anything?

(The three men look sadly at each other, and at the kids.)

Taylor: I'm afraid we must, Brian. We can keep you kids separated here at church, but if you're really going to learn better manners, your parents are the ones to teach you.

Steve *(jumps up in anger):* My parents aren't going to do a thing to me over this! They'll probably think the whole thing is as stupid as I do! You're making a big deal out of nothing, and my parents won't care!

Wells: Well, if that's true, I really feel sorry for you, Son.

Steve: I'm not your son! And what do you mean, you feel sorry for me?

Wells: I would hope and pray that your parents care enough about you to go to the trouble to teach you better manners, among other things, and care enough to discipline you when you get out of line.

Steve *(confused and unsure of his position):* Huh?

Karen: Well, there's no question about *my* parents. They definitely care enough to punish *me!*

Brian: Mine too. *(Short pause):* And, I guess I deserve it.

Steve: You guys make me sick! You can stick around and kiss up to these guys if you want to, but I've had enough *(moves toward the door).* All this talk about getting along with everyone in the world and putting yourself in other people's shoes

15

is just a lot of hot air. I don't see anyone giving *me* any breaks in *my* life, or treating *me* with much courtesy! Maybe when I get a little respect, I'll feel more like dishing it out!

Beth *(jumps up and joins Steve by the door):* Yeah! How come adults are always talking about how "disrespectful" teenagers are? All we ever hear is "do this," or "do that"! Orders from parents, orders from teachers, and now orders from you guys! Well you won't catch *me* sitting with any of these wimps *(she motions to include the four still sitting),* because I won't even *be* here!

(She and Steve storm out of the room. The seven remaining are quiet for a moment—the kids are worried about what the men are going to do next, the men are thoughtful.)

Taylor: I'm real sorry about that outburst and even more sorry that Beth feels it's necessary to stay away from church. That's the *last* thing we wanted!

Karen: Oh, don't worry about her, Mr. Taylor, she'll be back. She always blows up like that, but she won't stay mad for long.

Julie: Anyway, her parents will make her come back.

Wells: Well I'm glad to hear that! I only hope Steve's parents will do the same!

Taylor: I guess you kids have had enough lecturing from us. I hope none of your parents will be too hard on you, but will help you to see the seriousness of this situation. As I said before, this world would be a mighty sorry place to live if everyone always acted on their own, selfish impulses—but I'm sure you all realize that by now.

(All the kids nod.)

Jones *(stands up and opens his arms and hands out to the kids):* Let's just have a short prayer together, and then let's part as friends.

(Everyone scrambles over chairs, around desks, etc., to join hands in a circle as the lights go down.)

END OF SCENE 2

ACT 2, SCENE 1

The stage is divided into three sections with the largest being the center section. Arrange your lighting so that each section can be lit separately. If the dividers between the center and side sections could be built so that they could swing back and forth (see illustration), this would aid in the scene changes. You might also want to position a movable curtain or screen in front of the center section until time to use it.

The smaller sections on either side are furnished to look

like the bedrooms of Beth and Steve. Beds should face the audience lengthwise, with a bedside table in front (closest to the audience). In Steve's room, a desk is also in front of the bed, closer to the edge of the stage. It could be on the other side of the room from the head of the bed.

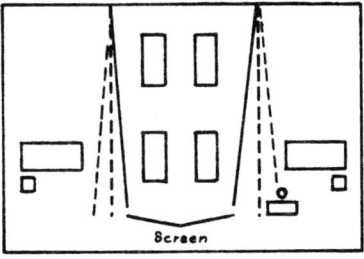

Beth is in her pajamas (dressed in school clothes underneath, but not so the audience can tell), sitting up in bed, talking on a telephone that is sitting on her nightstand. Steve is sitting at his desk, also talking on the telephone.

Beth: Man! Am I glad this day is over! I can't believe those three guys made such a big stink!

Steve: Yeah, it was pretty tense around here for a while. I didn't think my parents would get so uptight.

Beth: Well, if they're like mine, they were probably just embarrassed that an elder from the church came over to talk to them. My mother must have said "What will people think?" at least fifty times!

Steve: Yeah, my old man was pretty steamed at me, too. He didn't say much while Mr. Wells was here. But after he left, I got the whole bit about "I didn't raise any son of mine to be a hooligan!"

Beth (hoots with laughter): "Hooligan?!" Did he really say that?

Steve: Listen, my old man is a relic from the middle ages. Sometimes I get so sick of his stale, old jokes, I could just—well, you know, you've heard him!

Beth (sympathetically): Yeah, well, what can you do? We're stuck with the parents we've got! Did he ground you or anything?

Steve: No. Just blew out a lot of hot air—as usual.

Beth: I feel so sorry for Brian! He wasn't making as much noise as the rest of us, you know, but he's been grounded for a month! He's not even allowed to get any phone calls!

Steve: That's pretty stiff all right. Do you think his parents will hold him to it?

Beth: Probably—unless he gets time off for good behavior! They're really tough! I'd just *die* if my parents were that strict!

Steve: Yeah, it would be hard. Well listen Beth, I've gotta finish this calculus assignment before tomorrow.

Beth: Can't you just get your mom to write you an excuse?
Steve: Not after today! Besides, I've turned in so many excuses and missed so many of Stevenson's classes—I'll be lucky if I pass as it is. Looks like I'm really going to have to learn some of this junk.
Beth: Oh. OK then. Well, see ya.
Steve: Yeah. Bye.
Beth: Bye.
(Both hang up. Beth turns out her light and snuggles down under her covers. The lights go down on that section of the stage. Steve picks up a pencil and begins leafing through, occasionally reading, his calculus book. From the darkness comes Beth's sleepy voice:)
Beth: I *still* don't get what Mr. Jones meant about manners helping us to get along in the world ... I think he's just a dried-up old man, full of old ideas. ...
(Pause. All is quiet on the stage. As Steve begins to speak, Beth slips quietly offstage and out of her pajamas. She goes around to the left side to be ready for her next entrance. Steve yawns, rests his head on one arm, propped on the desk and stares off into space. Then he chuckles to himself.)
Steve: Those three old geezers sure got themselves worked up today! Rude! Arrogant! Bad mannered! This world sure *would* be a mess if we were as awful as they *think* we are!
(Steve turns a page in his book, then yawns again, gets up and stumbles over to his bed where he falls asleep. Lights go down on his section of the stage and gradually come up on the center section to reveal a school cafeteria.)

END OF SCENE 1

ACT 2, SCENE 2

The cafeteria has several rows of bare tables, ends toward the audience, with different-sized groups of kids scattered around. The kids either have school lunch trays, or bag lunches. At the center table, the two end seats (closest to the audience) are empty. In the next few seats, Josh, Todd, Erica, and Lee Ann are having lunch together. The boys are on the left side of the table, the girls on the right. To make the transition between scenes short, these kids can already be in place during the previous scene. As the lights come up, they will begin a background chatter that will continue (quietly!) throughout the scene. Beth enters from the left, carrying a tray with a school lunch on it. She glances around the cafeteria, then spies the bunch near the front. She walks over and plops her tray down next to Todd.

Beth: Hi, guys! Mind if I sit with you? *(She is already pulling the chair out when Erica answers.)*
Erica *(coldly)*: Would it make any difference to you if we said we did?
(Beth is momentarily taken aback, but then she recovers with an uncomfortable laugh, and sits down.)
Beth: Very funny, Erica! You're a barrel of laughs!
Lee Ann: So who's kidding? We *were* having a private conversation!
Erica: Yeah! And besides that, the only reason you want to sit here is because none of your stupid church friends are around, or because you want to flirt with Todd!
Beth *(hurt)*: Come on you guys! Gimmie a break—that's not true! I've eaten with you before, and, and, I've never flirted with Todd, *(pleadingly)* right Todd?
Todd: So who would notice? I wouldn't go out with you if you were the last girl on earth—the last girl in the universe!
Beth *(is stunned. She looks around the group and they return stony glares. Finally she says):* Hey! This is a joke, right? What's going on here?
Josh *(stands up and starts gathering his lunch stuff together):* Give it a rest, Morgan! If you can't take the hint that we don't want you around, I guess we'll have to make it a little more clear—come on you guys!

Just after Josh starts his speech and the others realize that he is leaving, they also start gathering their lunches together. The girls may stand while he is talking, but Todd should wait, so that he does not stand between Josh and the audience. Todd can push his chair back violently and noisily when Josh says "come on!" The four of them take their trays, books, purses, etc. and go to another table, glaring at Beth as long as possible. She is absolutely stunned for a while, then embarrassed. She looks around to see if anyone has noticed, and finds that several kids nearby are whispering, pointing at her, and laughing. She ducks her head and becomes very busy with her lunch, but she fumbles and drops things because she is so upset and embarrassed. The kids near her laugh louder. Just as Beth is about to throw in the towel, Steve comes in from the right, looking rather despondent himself, and walks over to the table where Beth is sitting.)

Steve: Hi Beth. *(Beth looks up in pleased surprise as Steve glances around the cafeteria.)* Where is everybody?
Beth *(rises half out of her chair and reaches across the table to grab at Steve's arm and lunch bag):* Steve! Oh man, am I glad

to see you! Hey! Sit down, will ya? Have a seat, pull up a chair, take a load off your feet!

Steve *(pulls back from her):* Hey! take it easy, will ya? You don't have to pull my arm outta socket! *(Pulls out the chair and sits, mumbling to himself):* But I must say, it's nice to hear that *somebody* wants me around!

Beth: Huh? What'd you say? *(Steve starts to answer, but Beth interrupts):* You wouldn't *believe* what just happened to me!

Steve: *You?* You wouldn't believe *my* whole day! I think the whole world's gone crazy!

Beth: You're kidding! That's just what I was going to say! Something really weird is going on here!

Steve *(begins to really pay attention for the first time):* What are you talking about, Beth? What's going on?

Beth: Everybody's been treating me like I'm from another planet all day long! My mother bit my head off this morning because I didn't hang up my towel after my shower, and then old Mrs. Robins threatened to call the *police* on me because I cut across her yard, and I can't get anyone here *(gestures around the cafeteria)* to even *talk* to me!

(Steve's mouth has been dropping wider and wider throughout this speech and he hasn't touched his lunch.)

Steve *(leans closer to Beth and says incredulously):* That's *exactly* what's been happening to *me* today! My mother got me out of bed at *5:30* this morning and made me go to the all-night market for milk, just because I forgot to bring some home yesterday! And then in calculus, I tried to ask Stevenson a question and he reamed me out—in front of everybody! He made this big speech about how he wasn't teaching for my personal convenience, and if I couldn't pay attention, I shouldn't waste his time with stupid questions. He said he wasn't getting paid enough to tutor every student individually and then he said, *(mockingly)* "Besides, I don't *feel* like answering your question!" Can you believe it?

Beth *(has been dropping her mouth wider and wider throughout this speech):* Awesome!

Steve: And that's not all! I didn't know *what* was going on with Stevenson, so I turned to David Powers—who sits next to me, you know?—and before I could say a *word,* he got on my case too! "Don't look at me," he said, "I'm certainly not going to tutor you! And I'm sick and tired of you wasting time in class! There are a few of us here who'd like to *learn* something!" And Beth, *everybody* in the *room* nodded and agreed with him! *(Beth shakes her head, mouth still open.)* It was

incredible! I felt like I was in the twilight zone!
(Beth's eyes widen and she leans toward Steve.)
Beth *(excitedly):* That's it! We must be in a time warp or something! Maybe we're a part of some weird experiment or something! I bet—
Steve *(disgustedly interrupts her):* Oh grow up! Get real, will you?
Beth *(hurt):* Well, I was only trying to figure it out! *(Pause.)* Hey, *(pleadingly)* don't you turn on me, too! I feel like you're the only friend I've got left in the world.
Steve *(gruffly):* Well, don't push your luck! *(mumbles under his breath):* Time warp! *(Then he glances nervously around the cafeteria.)* But *something* weird is going on, that's for sure!
Beth *(looks around too):* Yeah.
(They settle down to eating their lunches. Julie and Matt come in from the right and when Beth sees them, she brightens up considerably.)
Beth *(calls to them across the room):* Hey Julie! Hey Matt! Over here!
(Steve brightens up too, and turns to wave. Julie and Matt come over to the table but stop just behind Steve, who has turned to face them.)
Matt *(in anger):* What do *you* want? Haven't you two gotten us in *enough* trouble?
(At the first sound of his voice, Steve and Beth are visibly shaken.)
Julie: I've never been so embarrassed in all my life as I was yesterday, and you just *couldn't* let well enough alone, could you? Noooo! *(Shakes here finger at them): You* had to be a couple of tough guys! Well you just go ahead and stay tough, and stay rude, but *I'm* not getting into any more trouble because *you* can't learn when to shut up!
(Julie stomps off, stage left, with Matt close behind her. Steve and Beth are stunned into silence again. Slowly Beth turns back from watching them leave and faces Steve again.)
Beth *(incredulously):* Can you believe it?
Steve *(slowly shakes his head):* Maybe ... maybe some chemicals got into the water supply. *(Pause, then more excitedly):* Maybe the Russians are trying to make us kill each other off!
Beth *(disgustedly):* Oh come on, man! That's as dumb as my twilight zone theory!
Steve *(mumbles):* Yeah, I guess so. . . .
(Lights go down on cafeteria.)

END OF SCENE 2

ACT 2, SCENE 3

Stage hands can take a few seconds to adjust moveable walls, bedroom furniture, screen in front of center section, etc. This will give Beth time to leave through back of cafeteria (could be a space between the dividers) as soon as the lights go down.

Lights come up on Beth's bedroom. She is searching through dresser drawers for something and is angry about not finding it. From offstage, her mother's voice can be heard calling to Beth repeatedly. The longer she calls, the angrier she gets, and the more agitated Beth gets. Finally, after throwing clothes all over the floor, Beth starts toward the door of her room, just as her mother comes in.

Mom *(is furious):* Did you, or did you not, hear me calling you?

Beth: Yes, Mom, I heard you—I was just come—

Mom: *(mockingly):* "You were just ..." I get so tired of chasing after you kids and getting no help around here—do you think I have nothing better to do than to run all the way up here to remind you of jobs you're supposed to be doing anyway?

Beth *(exasperated, frustrated, and tired):* Mom, I'm sorry. I *was* on my way down to see what you wanted, but I have just had such an awful day—

Mom *(interrupts sarcastically):* Oh you poor dear! And I supposed you think I've been lying out in the sun all day?

Beth: No Mom, I didn't mean anything like that! But I wish you'd just listen a minute—

Mom: Well if that isn't the icing that takes the cake! I've been calling for you till my face turns blue, and now *you* want *me* to listen!

(Beth gives up. She slumps down dejectedly on her bed, sighs, then looks up at her mother.)

Beth: I'm sorry I didn't come when you called, Mother. What do you want?

Mom *(barely mollified):* I *want* you to come down and help me with dinner—as you're supposed to do without being told! I know you think God put me on earth to be your servant, but you're dead wrong about that! There are other things I'd like to do with my time besides be a chauffeur, cook, and cleaning lady for you and your brothers. *(Beth gets up from the bed and starts toward her bedroom door. Her mother turns to follow and shakes her finger at Beth's back.)* Of course it's too much to expect a word of thanks now and then. After all, one isn't expected to thank a servant for anything.

(They leave the stage with Beth's mother scolding her all the way. Then the lights go down on Beth's room, and come up on Steve's.)

Steve enters his bedroom, throws his books onto the desk, and throws himself down on his bed.)

Steve *(exhausted):* I don't believe this *whole* day! *(Lies quietly for a few seconds, then sits up on the bed, brings one foot up and begins untying his shoe. His father bursts into the room.)*

Dad *(angrily):* Where have you been?! You missed dinner and now I get home at nine o'clock and find that yard *still* unmowed!

Steve *(slaps his hand to his head):* Oh man, Dad, I forgot about the yard! But I *called* Mom and told her—

Dad *(interrupts, shouting):* You forgot?? You forgot!! You've been forgetting since last Wednesday! And where have you been since school let out?

Steve: Well, I called Mom and told her I was going to the library to study. Then Beth came to the library to help me with my calculus—and I guess I just forgot about the time.

Dad Right! You expect me to believe that you were at the *library, studying,* for *five* hours??

Steve: Really Dad! I'm way behind in calculus, and we're having a quiz tomorrow, and Old Man Stevenson is on my case, and—

Dad: "Old Man Stevenson"?? Is that how you refer to your teachers these days? Not in *this* house, buddy! And just why are you behind? Certainly not because you've been mowing the lawn instead of studying!

Steve: Look Dad, I'm really sorry—

Dad: Don't you "look Dad" me! You've tried to get out of mowing the lawn every week, and I'm sick of your excuses! I've got a good mind to make you go out and mow it *now!*

Steve: But Dad, it's *dark* outside!

Dad: Just another excuse! I would make you do it now but the neighbors would probably complain of the noise! But I'll tell you one thing, if that yard isn't mowed by the time I get home tomorrow—

Steve: I'll do it Dad, I will! It's just that—

Dad: I've heard *that* before! Now no more excuses! You get that yard mowed tomorrow, *or else!* And get your shoe off that bedspread! *(Storms out of the room, mumbling, "Kids act like money grows on trees. ...")*

Steve *(lifts one hand toward his dad, and starts to get up):* But Dad ... you didn't let me explain. ...

(Drops his arm, slumps back down on the bed and drops his head to his chest as the lights go down on his room.)

END OF SCENE 3

ACT 2, SCENE 4

Still in the bedrooms. Light comes up just a little on Beth's room as her alarm clock goes off. As the scene progresses, the light can gradually increase to full. Beth wakes up and rolls over to shut off the alarm. Then she props herself up on one elbow, facing the audience.)

Beth: Boy! I sure hope today is gonna be a better day than yesterday was! *(She lets out a big sigh.)*
(Beth's mom sticks her head in through the bedroom doorway, from the right.)
Mom *(normal tone of voice, maybe a little worried):* Beth? Are you up yet? It's already 7:30!
Beth *(very nervous and anxious, throws back the covers in a hurry):* OK Mom! I was just getting up! I'll be right down! Just need a few minutes to wash and get dressed!
Mom *(chuckles):* Well don't give yourself a heart attack! I'm sure I can save enough of the pancake batter to make you a couple when you come down!
Beth *(very surprised, perched on the edge of her bed):* Pancakes? You're gonna make pancakes for *me?*
(Mom comes into the room with a puzzled expression on her face. She sits down on the bed next to Beth.)
Mom *(lovingly):* What's the matter with you, you silly goose? Do you think I'd make pancakes for the rest of the family and not give you any?
Beth *(hesitantly):* Well, after what happened yesterday, I wasn't sure ...
Mom: Oh Beth! Your dad and I are very disappointed in you—misbehaving like that at your age—and I *was* really embarrassed to have Ralph Taylor come over here yesterday, to talk to us about your conduct—but I'm not going to punish you by taking away your *food!* Merciful heavens girl, what *can* you be thinking?
Beth *(very puzzled):* Mr. Taylor was here *yesterday?* You mean yesterday was Sunday?
Mom: Beth, your brain must still be asleep! Of course yesterday was Sunday—*(she does a Groucho Marx imitation)* and a very troublesome Sunday it was!
Beth *(as the light dawns on her face):* Oh Mom! I've just had the most awful nightmare! I thought yesterday was Monday, and—oh Mom, it was really awful!
Mom *(pats Beth on the knee):* Well, I'm sorry sweetie, but everything's OK now, isn't it?

Beth: I guess so. . . .
Mom: Well hurry up then, or you *will* be late for school. *(She starts toward the door.)* I'll go mix up that pancake batter.
Beth: Uh, Mom?
Mom *(from doorway)*: Yes?
Beth: Ummm, well, *(pause)* just thanks for checking to see if I was awake . . . and thanks for making pancakes. *(Mom looks very puzzled and surprised.)* Well, what I mean is, you do an awful lot of nice things for me, and I hardly ever say "thank you."
Mom *(jokingly)*: Oh sure you do, Beth! I get a card once a year on Mother's Day! *(Beth's head and shoulders drop and she looks miserable. Mom rushes over, sits down next to her again and puts her arm around her.)* Oh Beth, I'm sorry! I was just teasing—I didn't realize you were so serious! My! That must have been some nightmare!
Beth *(begins to cry)*: Mom, it was just awful! Everyone was so mean! So, so *rude!* I couldn't get *anyone* to help me, or speak kindly to me, and Mom, *(sobs)* I finally realized that that's the way I usually treat people! How can anyone *stand* me?
Mom *(hugs Beth to her as Beth continues to cry)*: Oh Beth, oh Honey, *(pats her)* that must have been awful! But don't you see? You dreamed all that stuff because of the lecture you got from the elders, and that's *good!* It just means that you did learn something after all! You're *not* always the easiest person in the world to get along with, *(Beth sobs)* but Honey, you're young, you have time to change! It's the people who remain rude and insensitive their whole lives who I feel sorry for! *(Takes Beth face into her hands)*: Beth, most teenagers go through a stage when they think it's cool to be rude—your concern over this just shows me that you are growing up—and I'm proud of you!
Beth *(collapses into fresh tears)*: Oh Mom! I *want* you to be proud of me! And from now on, I'm going to act like somebody you *can* be proud of!
(Mom and Beth hug and Mom wipes a tear from her own eye.)
Mom: I believe you will! And, I'm looking forward to it. But honey, now we've *really* got to get moving! *(They part. Mom stands up, Beth reaches for a tissue.)*
Beth: OK Mom, I'll hurry. And Mom?
Mom *(from doorway)*: Yes?
Beth Just . . . thanks.
Mom *(shaking her head)*: My! I wonder how we could get your brothers to dream that dream?

(Beth smiles sheepishly and Mom returns her smile as lights go down on Beth's bedroom, and up on Steve's.)

(Steve's alarm goes off, he groans, shuts it off and moves very slowly to a sitting position on the edge of his bed. Then he puts his face in his hands, elbows on knees, and sits there, shaking his head once in awhile. Soon, his dad pops his head through the door and says:)

Dad *(cheerily):* Up and at'em, my boy! If the bedbugs don't get you, the early birds will! *(As Steve lifts his head from his hands, Dad throws his hands up in a protective manner and says:)* Hold it, hold it! Don't jump all over me! I know how much you hate my "corny old-man jokes." I'll go, I'll leave you to your grumpy self!

Steve: No Dad, wait! I was just thinking how nice it is to hear you crack a joke—even if it *is* corny.

Dad *(comes through the doorway, faking a heart attack):* What?!? *(Stumbles up against the wall:)* Are my ears deceiving me? Can this be *Steve*, my son Steve? What's gotten into to you?

Steve: Aw Dad, it's not so strange. After yesterday, I just wasn't expecting you to crack a joke this morning, and it was kinda nice to hear—that's all.

Dad *(quits fooling around):* Well, yesterday *was* the pits, but your mother and I hope you've learned your lesson.

Steve *(amazed):* You mean you did all that—you and Mom acted like *that* to teach me a lesson?

Dad: Acted like what? *(Pats his chest):* I thought we were pretty cool! After all, it's not everyday that two elders come to visit, bearing miserable tales of our own son—and you hadn't even showed up from church yet! Didn't we stand by you when you finally did get home?

Steve: *That* was yesterday?! What about. . . . But then when. . . . *(Realization lights his face.)* Oh man, Dad, did I have an incredible dream! *(More realization.)* Yeah! You and Mom *were* really cool! And listen, I just want to thank you!

Dad: Well, we figured you had been embarrassed enough, being dragged out of—*(stops abruptly)* —what did you say?

Steve: I said, "thanks!" I appreciate the fact that you and Mom didn't get on my case. Well, I mean, I realize now that I *should* appreciate it, because of what happened yester—I mean last night. *(Dad just stands there, looking dumbfounded. Steve stands up, goes over to him, and puts his hand on his shoulder, the one furthest from the audience.)* Listen Dad, what I'm trying to say is, I really have learned my lesson—thanks for not embarrassing me anymore in front of those guys, and . . . *(drops his hand and becomes nervous)*, well, I really don't mind your corny jokes, only—I sorta wish you'd go easy on 'em around my friends, but really Dad *(rushing his words now)*, it's OK if you want to clown around, cuz I really don't mind, cuz, well, I'd rather have you *that* way than some other ways you could be, and, well, I guess I'm just glad that you are the way you are!

(Both men are embarrassed, neither knows what to expect next.)

Dad: *(solemnly):* That's quite a speech, Son. Uh, what's wrong? Are you in some kind of trouble?

Steve *(frustrated):* No Dad! What happened yesterday just got me to thinking—about getting along in this world and all—and then I had this awesome dream! A nightmare, really! And then when you popped in here this morning, I was just so glad to be given another chance—*(Dad frowns, looks puzzled)*—I mean, I'm glad to be here, and I'm glad you're the way you are!

Dad: You're too deep for me this morning! Look, whaddya say you hurry up and get dressed, and I'll drop you off at school on my way to work?

Steve *(enthusiastically):* That'd be great, Dad! *(Starts moving rapidly around the room, throwing clothes on the bed, etc.)* I need to get to school early anyway. I need to talk to Mr. Stevenson, and I can't wait to tell Beth about my dream— *(stops to call to Dad, who is almost out of the room)*, and Dad?

Dad *(turning around):* Yes?

Steve *(grinning):* Thanks a lot!

Dad *(shakes his head, studies Steve):* You're welcome, Son, and thank *you!* Your manner this morning has given new meaning to my day! *(He grins and Steve grins back as lights go down.)*

CURTAIN

DISCUSSION QUESTIONS

1. The words used to describe behavior can have a heavy emotional impact. How would the kids feel if the elders called them "rude"? How would they feel if the elders said they were being "insensitive to the people around them"? Is being insensitive always the same thing as being rude?

2. Attitudes play a major role in behavior. In the beginning of the play, what attitude did the kids display toward God? What was their attitude toward the people around them? What was Beth's attitude toward her mom when her mom was calling her? What attitude did her mom *think* Beth was displaying? Steve's dad also assumed that Steve was disobeying him, making up excuses, not being honest. Why? Do parents just automatically think the worst of their kids? What may have happened before to cause Beth's mom and Steve's dad to be so suspicious?

3. Mr. Wells said that good manners were a way of showing respect for other people's rights and feelings. Do you agree with that definition? If our society operated totally without respect for one anothers rights, what would the environment be like? Are laws made to protect individual rights? If everyone could be counted on to always act in a courteous and mannerly way, could we do away with some of those laws?

4. We don't have laws to protect personal feelings, unless you consider "unwritten" laws or what is known as "common courtesty," or "societal rules." Since these types of rules vary from country to country, behavior that is considered polite in one country can create a very bad impression in another. What behavior is considered polite in this country—what kind of things are we expected to do (or not do) in order to avoid offending others?

5. While we don't have laws governing our speech, we do have instruction from God. Read James 3:1—12 and 4:11—17. What kinds of "rules" do you find there? Do you have control over your tongue? Do you know anybody who does?

6. Because the teenage years are a time of finding and creating new identities, developing new freedoms and responsibilities, many teens feel that they are in a battle against parents, teachers, and other authority figures. Do you think this battle is real or imagined? Are authority figures trying to keep teens from growing up, from accepting new responsibilities? What causes some teens to feel that they must rebel against authority? This rebellion—or need to assert one's own independence—is often expressed in rudeness. Is being rude an effective way to express individuality?

7. One of the biggest problems with being rude—either intentionally unkind or carelessly insensitive—is that rudeness invites misunderstanding and rudeness in return. Have you ever known anyone to get into this vicious cycle? Without intending to, people can get into a cycle of rudeness that almost becomes a habit and is almost always expected. How can people—families especially—break such a habit? Is the reverse true—do soft words invite soft words in return? Does kindness invite kindness? What does Proverbs 15:1 say about this?

FRACTURED FAMILIES

CAST OF CHARACTERS
Karen Kersteen
Kristi Kersteen
Rob Witter
Dave Williams
TJ (Tommy James)
Patti Thompson
Larson, male or female homeroom teacher
Simon, male or female guest lecturer
Ross, male or female guest lecturer
> Simon and Ross carry the bulk of this play. They should be good actors or actresses who can carry the dialogue quickly and with great enthusiasm. They need to be friendly, effervescent types who are able to establish a quick rapport with kids and adults.

Prentice, male or female principal of school
Mr. and Mrs. Kersteen, Karen and Kristi's parents
Mr. and Mrs. James, TJ's parents
Mr. and Mrs. Witter, Rob's parents, have no lines
Mr. Thompson, Patti's dad
Mr. and Mrs. Williams, Dave's parents, have no lines

SCENES
Act 1: Hallway outside the school's auditorium.
Act 2: School classroom
Act 3, Scenes 1 and 2: School gymnasium

ACT 1

Large set of auditorium doors from which kids are exiting into a school hallway. (Auditorium doors, lockers, and a closed door to a classroom painted on a backdrop will provide all the setting you need.) These kids can be various ages in junior and senior high school. Two girls (sisters—could be twins) come toward the edge of the stage and stop to talk. Other kids continue exiting in both directions. Most are carrying some combination of schoolbooks, notebooks, purses, etc.

Karen: Well *that* was the most depressing assembly I've ever sat through!

Kristi: Oh Karen, it wasn't supposed to be depressing—just informative!

Karen: Right. All you ever wanted to know about teenage suicide, but were too depressed to ask!

Kristi: Oh you! You always see the negative side of things!

Karen: Better watch me—that's one of the warning signals! I may be ready to cash in my chips!

Kristi: It isn't a laughing matter! According to that movie, fifteen teenagers kill themselves every day.

Karen: Yeah, yeah. I heard. And that doesn't include the accidental deaths from drugs, drinking, and reckless driving. *Now* who's being negative?

Kristi: Well, I just don't think you should joke about it.

(Rob and Dave walk up from the door and join the girls.)

Rob *(to Dave in a game show host voice):* And now, for the grand prize, how did the Kersteen girls react to this morning's assembly?

Dave *(excitedly):* I've got it! I've got it! Karen thought it was *toooo* depressing and Kristi feels *soooo* sorry for those teens who tend toward suicide!

(The two girls stand open-mouthed for a minute and then Kristi speaks.)

Kristi *(semi-angry):* Humph! You're only half right! I didn't say *anything* about feeling sorry for them—only that it's a very serious matter. *(Pause. Curiously:)* How'd you know that?

Dave and Rob: Ha!

Dave: We knew it because we know you so well.

Rob *(doing a Groucho imitation):* And we know you so well because we like you so much!

(Both girls grin and are pleased with the comment.)

Karen *(doing Groucho back):* Oh, a couple of wise guys, huh? *(Regular voice):* Well, what did *you* think about it?

Dave: It was pretty depressing.

Rob: But you gotta feel sorry for those kids.

Kristi *(laughing):* Oh, cut it out!

Rob: Well seriously, I thought it contained some useful information. I guess I'm just tired of hearing about it. If you'd never contemplated suicide, you might after three or four TV specials and a couple of guest lecturers at school!

Dave: Your problem is, you're just too well-adjusted. Now if you'd been through some of the traumas some kids here have—

Rob: Stick to one subject at a time, Dave. Am I well-adjusted or just never had any problems?
Karen: You know he had to face the death of his father.
Kristi: And his mother's remarriage.
Dave: Yeah, right. Well, on a well-adjusted scale from one to ten, with ten being the best, I'd give him a twenty-four. *(All laugh.)*
Kristi: That describes Rob all right!
Karen: Yeah. How'd you get to be so cotton-pickin' cheerful?
Rob: You want a serious answer or what?
(Tommy James joins the group.)
TJ: A serious answer about what? How many kids are gonna go home and try it now that we've learned the most successful methods?
Kristi: Oh TJ, what a terrible thing to say! No, we were just wondering how come Rob's always so cheerful—losing his father and all.
TJ: You lost your dad? How'd you manage that? *(Sarcastically.)* I'd like to lose mine sometime!
(There is an embarrassed silence for a moment.)
Rob *(kindly):* My father died when I was ten, TJ
TJ: Oh. Ahh, I'm sorry man. I guess my mouth got in the way of my brains again.
Rob: No problem. It was a long time ago and I'm over it.
TJ *(trying to make amends):* Ahh, do you miss him?
Rob: Sometimes. I like to think about the times we had together. But he was so sick at the end that it would have been cruel to have wanted him to live. Besides, my mom married another terrific guy two years later, and now *he's* a terrific dad. She sure can pick 'em!
TJ: Some guys get all the luck!
Dave: Why do you say that?
TJ: I can't stand my dad but I'll probably be stuck with him all my life. Rob, on the other hand, has had *two* great fathers.
Karen: Hummm. Wonder if it has anything to do with the kind of son you are?
Kristi: Karen! What an awful thing to say! You should apologize to TJ right now!
TJ: Why? I don't feel insulted.
Karen: No, it's not an insult, just an observation. See, our dad has an optimist like Rob—that's you, and a pessimist like TJ—that's me, and our dad's about half wonderful—
Dave *(laughing):* And half what? You kill me, Karen! What a dumb theory.

Rob: I don't see why it's so dumb. If parents influence their kids personalities, why not the other way around? Hey, that'd make an interesting experiment.

Patti *(joining the group):* What would? Trying to get your parents to come to this ridiculous rap session? No way my parents will come!

Rob: Why do you say that?

Kristi: How do you know until you ask them?

Patti: In the first place, my mother is living in (name some city far from yours) with her boy friend, and in the second place, my father is so busy with his job that he doesn't have time to talk to *me*, let alone come to some group session. Besides, even if he did come, he wouldn't say anything, so what good would it do?

Dave: He might learn something from just listening. I think that's the whole idea behind these groups.

Patti: Oh, I'm sure it would be useful, but he won't come so it won't do me any good.

TJ: Right. You guys don't know what it's like to have parents who couldn't care less about you—mine would never participate in one of these rap sessions either.

Karen: Why not?

TJ: Even if they would admit that our family has problems, which they won't, they'd never talk about 'em because that's "airing your dirty laundry in public."

Patti: Yeah. and if you do that, you'd have to admit to everybody that you're not perfect, and my dad would never do that!

Karen: Hummm. Well if everybody feels that way, there won't be *any* discussion going on.

Kristi: On the other hand, sometimes a group will give you the courage to say things you wouldn't say face to face. I mean, you know your parents aren't going to climb all over you in public for something you say.

Rob: Right! The moderators won't allow that! Of course, they won't let *us* get away with anything either! Besides, I'll bet these counselors really know what they're doing—they probably have ways of bringing things out without hurting any feelings!

Dave: Yeah. I'm really looking forward to the "talk training" we're going to get before the rap session. Even in the best of families, and mine is pretty ... OK—*(Everybody laughs.)* — even we could use some lessons in communication skills.

Patti: Yeah, it all sounds great. I wish my dad would come—

Kristi: Hey! Maybe the pre-rap-session talk training will show you a special way to invite him!
Rob: Yeah! I'll bet it will!
Patti: Well ... we'll see. I'm not gettin' my hopes up.
TJ: Me neither. But it *would* be nice. *(Pause.)* Listen, I gotta go. See you guys tomorrow. *(Starts to leave.)*
Patti: Wait a sec, TJ, I'll walk with you. *(To others):* See ya!
Others: OK, bye, see you tomorrow. Bye Patti, Bye TJ, etc.
Karen: That's pretty sad, isn't it? Makes me sorry that I complain about my parents so much. At least they're still together, and I know they love me.
Dave: That's a *lot* to be thankful for! My parents may be together, but sometimes I wonder why they are, and why they ever bothered to have kids. Do you know, in all my life—at least as far back as I can remember—neither of my parents have ever told me that they love me? I'm pretty sure they do, but it would sure be nice to hear it!
Kristi: Have you ever told them that you love them?
Dave: Are you kidding? We just don't *do* that in our family!
Rob: Bet you'd knock their socks off if you did, huh?
Dave: Sure! My mom would think I was after something and my dad would think I was turning weird on him!
Rob: That's really too bad. I don't know how I would make it without knowing that Mom and Dad love me.
Karen: Do they just come right out and tell you that?
Rob: Sure. Almost everyday.
Others: Wow!
Kristi: Maybe *that's* why you're always so cheerful—so well adjusted.
Rob: Well, that helps, for sure! But don't be too hard on your parents. A lot of people just aren't comfortable with expressions of love—verbal or physical—just because *they* didn't grow up with them.
Karen: So the cycle continues.
Kristi: Well, maybe it can be broken. Maybe we should just try it.
Karen: Ummm. Now you're talking scary!
Rob: It's worth the risk, I assure you! What do you think, Dave? Could you do it?
Dave: I dunno. I hope my parents will come to this thing though. Maybe if they saw how other parents relate—
Karen: Yeah, this could be a pretty good deal! *(Looks at her watch.)* Kristi, we'd better hit the road. Mom will be calling out the National Guard pretty soon.

Rob: See there? An expression of love! She worries about you when you're not home on time!

Karen: Oh come on—

Dave *(breaking in):* Yeah, that's right! My mom hardly ever asks me where I'm going or when I'll be back. Sometimes when I come home from school she'll say, "Are you here already?" Makes me feel like I should have stayed away longer!

(The others don't know whether to laugh or be sympathetic. They do a little of both.)

Kristi: Sorry Dave! That's kinda funny, but I know it hurts, too. Listen! I'm gonna pray that this talk training and rap session really open things up for you, and for us, too.

Dave *(incredulous):* Pray?! You'll pray for *me?*

Rob: Sure! That's a great idea. I will too! You know it has to be God's will that families have good communication!

Dave: Oh yeah? Well if it's God's will, how come every family doesn't have it?

Rob: Because people have gone against God's will! *(Kiddingly.)* It's happened before, ya know. But if we pray for His will to happen, and make the changes in our own behavior that will allow it, great things will happen!

Karen: This is getting more and more exciting!

Kristi: Yeah, it is, but you're right about getting home—we'd better!

Rob: OK—see you two tomorrow.

Dave: Yeah, and thanks—thanks for saying you'd pray for me. No one's ever said that to me before.

Karen: No kidding?

Kristi: Well then, we'll have to continue this conversation another time! Bye!

All: Bye Dave, bye Rob, see ya, etc.

(The girls leave and after a moment, Dave speaks.)

Dave: Do you really believe all that stuff about God's will and prayer and stuff?

Rob: I sure do! I've seen what the power of prayer can do, and knowing God's will ... I guess that's what gives me peace in my life.

Dave: What do you mean?

Rob: I know that God loves me and that it is His will for my life to be worth something. So, as long as I don't turn my back on Him, I can be pretty confident that no matter what career I choose, or where I spend my life, it will count. God will use me for something good! That gives me a pretty good feeling inside.

Dave: Yeah, I can see how it would. *(Pauses.)* Listen, is it God's will for everyone's life to be worth something?

Rob *(claps his arm around Dave's shoulders as they start down the hall):* It sure is, Buddy! But before God can start making your life worthwhile, you have to turn it over to Him by your own free will. See, God doesn't force anyone to do anything, so until you turn your life over to Him ... *(Lights go down as the boys walk off.)*

END OF ACT 1

ACT 2

School classroom. All the kids from Act one are there, plus some extras. Homeroom teacher is present with two adult guests. They can be any combination of males and/or females that you wish. Kids are all talking to each other as the lights come up.

Larson: OK, kids, let's get this show on the road. *(They quiet down, turn around to face front, put away purses, etc.)* Our two guests are from the University of (name your state) where they are studying family communication problems, and how they relate to the teenage suicide problem. We don't know that any of you are contemplating suicide *(pauses and surveys the room),* but whether you are or not, solving communication problems at home would probably improve your life. Am I right? *(Positive response from class.)* OK. So these two are going to give you a head start on tonight's rap session with your parents by teaching you some keys to conversation. So listen up. Who knows? You and I might even learn to communicate better!

(The kids laugh as Simon and Ross move into place.)

Simon: Good morning, and thanks for letting us speak to you today.

Ross: We're glad to be here and happy to be able to give you some help in communicating with your parents.

Simon: In a way, our meeting with you first is a little unfair, because we're going to ask your parents to follow the same communication rules.

Ross: But we've found that a little advance notice gives you time to practice the principles—

Simon: And if you spring 'em on your parents tonight, they may be shocked into dropping their guards! *(Laughter.)*

Ross: We're going to use a little acronym to help you remember the communication keys. *(Notices puzzled looks on* *students' faces.)* Oh yes, you know what an acronym is. You've just momentarily forgotten.

Simon: An acronym is a word formed by taking the first letter from each word in a series. You then use that word to help you remember the series of words.

(Kids nod and say, "Oh yeah," "Right," etc.)

Simon: Sure, we knew you knew that! *(Some laughter.)*

Ross: Our acronym is GET REAL. (It would be good to have some kind of visual aid for Simon and Ross to use at this point. Either a chalkboard, or overhead projector, or a big pre-drawn chart which could be uncovered bit by bit.) What we hope you and your parents will do with each other is "get real," and here are some ways to do it.

Simon: The "G" stands for, "grow up." *(Laughter.)* That's what you're gonna have to do if you want your parents to get real with you. *(Some kids start to protest. Simon holds up his hands and says,)* Oh I know, I know. Some of your parents need to grow up, too. Well, don't worry, we'll get them tonight. *(Laughter.)*

Ross: What we want *you* to do when we tell you to grow up is to stop thinking you must have your own way all the time. You're big kids now, you *know* that isn't the way the world works.

Simon: Sometimes the answer is "yes," sometimes it's "no." So just grow up, will 'ya? *(Laughter.)*

Ross: Another aspect of growing up is realizing and accepting that your parents aren't perfect, and that is perfectly OK! Allow your parents to make a mistake once in a while—you'll appreciate it when they do the same for you.

Simon: This brings us straight to the second letter, "E," which stands for "ease up." Before you respond in your normal declaration-of-war fashion to your parents' request, stop and ask yourself, "Is this worth fighting over?" Ease up! Not everything in life is worth the emotion that is frequently attached to it. Ease up! When your mom tells you for the third time to clean your room, stop and remember that she wouldn't be nagging if you'd done it the first time!

Ross: "T" stands for "timing." You guys are old enough to know when is and when is not a good time to ask your parents to buy you a Maserati. *(The kids scream with laughter.)* If you've just brought home a report card containing three D's, it is not a good time. If your father just lost a promotion he was expecting and your mother just got a ticket for speeding, it is not a good time. Nor is it particularly good timing to ask your mother when she's stumbling through the door with an arm load of groceries, company's coming in thirty minutes and *you* forgot to take the meat out of the freezer as you were told. *(Kids laugh.)*

Simon: Use a little common sense. If you and your best friend just had a terrible fight, would you welcome your little sister's request to take her roller skating? No? *(Kids respond.)* Then give your parents the same courtesy.

Ross: Now we come to the "R," which stands for "repeat." Some of the best communication advice we can give you is to repeat what the other person just said to you. For example,

Simon: Did you say that it helps a conversation along to repeat what the other person said?

Ross: Yes! First of all, both parties are *sure* of the issue at hand. Secondly, if you've been surprised by a statement, repeating it gives you time to think of your best response.

Simon: Thirdly, repeating the statement makes it unequivocally clear that you are paying attention—which is a high compliment to your partner.

Ross: Fourthly, if your communication partner has just made a really stupid statement, repeating it to him will give him the opportunity to back down or modify the statement.

Simon: If you practice all of these rules, and there are many more, you will be well on your way to *earning* your parents' respect. This is really crucial and this is what the second "E" stands for. Many people, adults and teens alike, think that automatic, unconstrained respect is their due. We disagree. We may all start out on equal footing, but respect and disrespect are *earned*. If you want your parents to respect you as an adult, you've got to show them adult behavior and adult decisions.

Ross: And if you treat them disrespectfully, there is no way they are going to respect you!

Simon: "A" stands for "ask," and "assume," two entirely different hints. The first is to *ask* for your parents' advice, opinions, and feelings. They will be so surprised and flattered that they may adjust the advice they had planned to give you anyway! *(Laughter.)*

Ross: All kidding aside, this is not a trick. If you love your parents and want to open the communication lines, ask them how they feel about things in your life. Say, "Dad, I'd like to take chemistry and microbiology this semester, but I can take only one. Which do you think would be the most useful?"

39

Simon: Or how about this? "Mom, your hair always looks so nice. How can I get mine to do that?" *(Kids hoot and howl.)* Ridiculous you say? Wouldn't you pay that compliment to your best friend, and ask her advice? And wouldn't it be nice if your mom could be your best friend?

Ross: "A" also stands for "assume the best." We did that with you when we started this speech—do any of you remember how? *(Pauses, no response other than murmurings.)* We didn't expect you to remember because it is a very subtle attitude.

Simon: And that's *exactly* what it is—an attitude on your part that things will go well, that your request is reasonable and you expect a reasonable response. If you go into a conversation *assuming* the best, your attitude will have a subtle but powerful effect on the outcome. By the way, we did that with you by saying "thanks for letting us speak to you," and "we're happy to be able to give you some help." See? We *assumed* that you would listen, and we *assumed* that what we have to say would be of help to you!

Ross: Finally, the best communication key of all times: *listen!* Really listen to what is being said. Don't be daydreaming about that cute kid in your homeroom. Don't be planning your response before you've heard the whole point. *Listen* to your parents, *assume* that they have your best interest at heart, *earn* their respect by clearly *repeating* what they said.

Simon: Decide whether or not now is a good *time* to disagree, *ease up* on them by not demanding perfection, and

Simon and Ross *(in unison):* Grow up!

Ross: Don't play the part of an immature or spoiled kid. Don't give your parents reason to believe that you still need a babysitter. Because if you do, that's exactly how they'll treat you and *you won't like it!*

Simon: Hey! You've been a fantastic audience.

Ross: If your parents are half as responsive tonight, you all are on your way to some great conversations!

Simon: Now *practice* today; try these techniques with your friends and see if you, and they, don't feel better for it.

Ross: We'll see you tonight, with the rest of your classmates. In the meantime, let us leave you with words from the wisest philosopher of all times, King Solomon.

Simon: He said, "Reckless words pierce like a sword, but the tongue of the wise brings healing." Good-bye and good conversation!

(The kids break into applause. Simon and Ross wave as they leave the room. When the clapping dies down, Larson steps up.)

Larson: That was a pretty good speech, didn't you think so? *(Hands shoot up.)* Yes, Rob?

Rob: Thanks for asking my opinion, I respect you for that! *(Dave jumps right in.)*

Dave: Did you say you respect him because he asked your opinion?

(The room breaks up in laughter, including Larson.)

Larson: OK you clowns, the hour's up anyway. Have a great day, and best wishes for tonight.

(The kids begin to leave, talking excitedly, as the lights go down.)

END OF ACT 2

ACT 3, SCENE 1

The rap session will take place in the school gymnasium where students are grouped by homerooms. The only group we'll hear from will be our own, but others will be referred to. A backdrop could have another group painted on it, or you could recruit a bunch of extras to act like they're having a rap session too, but neither is necessary. A stage with one group of folding chairs will convey the idea. All of the students from the previous two scenes are present, with one or both parents. You could use a microphone as a prop for the speakers, but don't have it turned on or the other characters will sound odd. As the lights come up, Principal Prentice is coming to the mike. Use one side of your stage as the front of the gym.

Prentice: Good evening, students and welcome, parents. We're so glad to have you all here tonight, and this is a terrific turnout! I don't want to dwell on the depressing statistics but I do want to give you a brief background on this session.

As you are probably well aware, suicide is fast becoming the number one cause of death among teenagers. The National Bureau of Health statistics reports that 500,000 American teenagers will attempt suicide this year, and at least 5,000 will succeed. In their study of this problem, Mr./Ms. Simon and Mr./Ms. Ross from the University of _____ discovered an important unifying link. First of all, the *variables* surrounding teen suicides (divorce, physical illness, death of some loved one, being moved, etc.) are *not* the causes. Suicide occurs because of a teen's lack of self-esteem and self-worth. Secondly, the single most powerful factor to combat these feelings of worthlessness is a strong family relationship. Thirdly, the biggest obstacle to having that relationship is poor communication.

We who are in the field of education are here because we like kids. We like to watch them mature, we like to teach them, we like to think we've had some small part in every successful life. The faculty here at Riverside High was therefore delighted to hear of Simon and Ross' program to combat teenage suicide, and eager to invite them to come share with our students. And so, without further delay, here are Simon and Ross.

(Prentice steps aside as the audience applauds. The kids are applauding more enthusiastically than their parents, who have yet to be won over to this idea. Simon and Ross take the mike, or come to the front.)

Simon: Thank *you* for that warm reception! You know, we'd rather that teen suicide wasn't a problem in this country and we'd rather that all family members already knew how to express themselves to each other, but if that's not going to be the case, we can't think of a job we'd rather be doing than the one we're doing here tonight.

Ross: That's right. It is *extremely* gratifying to see teens and parents break down the hurdles that are keeping them apart. Especially since most of the time, those barriers are so STU-PID! *(Kids laugh, adults look nervous.)*

Simon: Your principal gave a good introduction; short and sweet. You see, that's really all there is to the problem. Kids feel worthless because the people who mean the most to them are not conveying worth to them.

Ross: We're sidestepping a word here, and I'll bet some of you have already guessed what it is ... hummm? When we talk about kids not feeling worthwhile and parents not conveying worth, what are we really talking about? *(A few kids suggest, "love?")*

That's right! Love. Ahhh! There's a scary subject, right? *(Affirmative, nervous response.)*

Simon: Well OK. Before we jump right into that, then, let's deal with another problem. I'll bet some of you kids were doubting today that your parents would come. *(Karen gives Patti a nudge and Rob gives the high sign to Dave, while Kristi is nodding to TJ.)*

Ross: And I'll bet some of you parents reluctantly agreed to come but promised yourself that you weren't going to participate. *(Parents grin sheepishly as they glance around at other parents. Kids are giggling and whispering.)*

Simon: Well, we *could* waste a lot of time trying to get you to break down your own private barriers but instead, we're just going to do it for you. *Now* we're going to jump right into that scarey subject called love.

Ross: In Mr. (Ms.) Prentice's introduction he (she) said that kids are killing themselves because they don't feel loved. He also said that parents were failing to communicate their love to their kids. The one single fact he (she) left out was that *all parents do love their kids.*

Simon: Oh, I know what you're thinking: "There have to be some parents that don't." Well, you may be right but we've got a big news flash for you: NONE OF THOSE PARENTS ARE HERE TONIGHT! You know how we know that?

Ross: Because you're here. You wouldn't have bothered to come if you didn't love your kids. So ... here's where we're going to take the first, the biggest, and the hardest step for you.

Simon: Parents, your kids *love* you, or they wouldn't have bothered to invite you here tonight. Furthermore, some of them have been sick at heart all day for fear you wouldn't come. They love you very much, and they want very much to be able to communicate that to you! *(All over the gym, parents and kids are shifting uncomfortably. Some look at each other, some don't. Others are comfortable and grin at each other.)*

Ross: Kids, now it's your turn. Your parents *love* you!! If just one of your parents is here tonight, that's OK. Maybe your missing parent has a legitimate reason for not being here, or maybe he or she wasn't around to receive the invitation. The most important thing is that the parent who *is* here, loves *you!* Furthermore, some of your parents accepted this invitation tonight thinking that it would do no good because they'll *never* be able to communicate with you, but they came anyway. They came because of that one, small chance that it might do some good and they love you enough to go for it. *(Audience responds as before, perhaps a little less uncomfortable—shy smiles, nods, knee pats, etc.)*

Simon: Now that we've taken the hardest step for you, it's your turn! *(Audience responds, "oh oh!", giggles, looks fearful, etc.)* To make it easier, we're going to do this in unison, but if you hold back, you'll be doing it alone, so you'd better jump right in there. We'll take the parents first because this might be somewhat less foreign to them.

Ross: Parents, on the count of three we want each of you to face your child, look him or her in the eye, call him or her by name, and say, "I love you." If you have more than one child here, turn and speak to the other, but don't you *dare* not do this. We all know that there is *far* too much at stake here to let self-conscious hang-ups get in the way. Ready? No time to backout! One, two, three. *(The parents do as they have been instructed. Some faces are screwed up with the effort to keep from crying. There is a soft rumble all over the stage with only a word now and then distinguishable. When it is over, parent and child are exchanging lopsided grins.)*

Simon: OK kids, your turn! *(Groans are heard.)* Don't give me that! I *know* better! *(During the rest of this speech, Simon's voice grows higher and higher and louder and louder to create a fever pitch of excitement.)* I know that some of you are just dying to do this. You've wanted to tell your parents for so long, but you didn't know how, and now you're being forced into it, and the love inside you is swelling up and building up and is just about ready to explode—NOW! Call them by name! Look into their eyes! One! Two! Three! *(The kids do as they have been instructed. The expressions are as before. The rumble is a little bit louder this time.)**

Ross *(yelling):* All right! Hey! How do you feel? *(Laughter—the tension breaks, parents and kids break into applause.)* OK! You know what you're feeling? That's called *relief!* *(Laughter.)* Now, why is it *so* hard to tell the ones we love that we love them?

Simon: Whatever the reason, we're over the hurdle. If you like that warm, bubbly feeling that's growing inside of you, if you're enjoying the sense of release that came with getting these three little words out into the open, do yourselves a favor; try them again on the way home tonight. Then try them in the morning before you go your separate ways. If you're *really* adventerous, try them in the middle of a fight! *(Laughter.)* But whatever you do, *don't* fail to use those words again. *(Seriously.)* As God is my witness, they are the most powerful words in the English language.

Ross: Now, you're already seated in groups according to your homerooms. This is to make the next section a little easier. We want you to do some sharing and the smaller groups should make you feel more comfortable about doing so.

Simon: We don't want you to feel forced to participate. If you just *cannot* bring yourself to join in the discussion, then at least take notes and have these conversations with your kids at home.

---

*You could tape record these events during rehearsals for playback during the performance, to make it sound like there are more groups participating.

Ross: But remember, we're all in the same boat here. We're all parents and teenagers who would like to be able to communicate better, so we really have nothing to hide.

Simon: We gave your kids some keys to communication earlier today which we will now give to you in the form of a handout. *(A couple of kids near Simon and Ross jump up and start passing out sheets of paper.)* We won't take time to go over these keys together, but they will provide you with something to discuss with your sons and daughters. They heard the full presentation and will be glad to share the rules with you! *(Laughter.)*

Ross: OK. Now, on the backside of that list of communication keys is a list of questions for parents, and a list for teens, designed to get you started in talking to one another. Not every person needs to answer every question—at least not here, and not tonight, *please! (Laughter.)* In your groups, speak out whenever you get an opportunity. To get things started we'll just ask that the person wearing the most blue speak first and then the person in the most purple. Experience has shown us that after that, things usually move right along.

Simon: Any questions? *(None.)* OK! Take it away, groups!

(Attention shifts to our group. Everyone is fidgity. Rob looks down at himself and sees that he's wearing blue jeans, a light blue shirt, and blue socks.)

Rob: Well, as luck would have it, I seem to be the one in blue! *(Light laughter from others.)* So, guess I'll take a crack at the first question. *(Looks at list and reads):* "What one thing about today has impressed you the most?" *(Thinks.)* Hummm. Well, as I told a couple of my friends this morning, my mom and dad often tell me they love me. By the way, this is my mom, Ruth Witter, and this is my step-dad, Jim Witter. My biological father died when I was ten, but Jim has been a real dad to me. As TJ pointed out to me this morning, I've been twice blessed. Anyway, to get back to what I was saying, it isn't odd or uncomfortable for us to tell each other that we love each other, and I guess I just realized today how unusual that is. It's one of those things that you take for granted until you see that not everyone is as lucky. *(Pause.)* Ummmm, Karen, you're wearing the most purple—do you want to take the same question, or the next one?

Karen: I'll do the same question because there *is* something that has made an impression on me. See—on this list of

45

communication keys *(they all turn their papers over)*, the "G" stands for "grow up." Mr. (Ms) Ross and Mr. (Ms.) Simon said this morning that part of growing up is realizing and accepting that your parents aren't perfect. ...
(Mr. and Mrs. Kersteen look at each other in surprise.)
Mr. Kersteen: Well, Karen, I think we can admit to that without too much loss of face. Heh, Heh! *(Others laugh politely.)*
Karen: Well, I don't have much trouble realizing that you're not perfect—I mean, don't take offense, *nobody* is.
Mrs. Kersteen: Then what impresses you about that statement?
Karen: I've been thinking about it all day, see, and there's something I don't get.
Mr. Kersteen: What's that?
Karen: Well, when I make a mistake, I'm expected to apologize for it. That's OK, that's the way it should be. After I apologize and you forgive me, the problem is pretty much over.
Mr. Kersteen: Right.
Karen: So how come when you make a mistake, you don't apologize to me? *(Mr. and Mrs. Kersteen are embarrassed.)*
Mrs. Kersteen: Well really now, Karen, I don't think it's your father's place to—*(Patti cuts in.)*
Patti: Why isn't it? *(Everybody looks at her in shock.)* Excuse me for buttin' in. I'm Patti Thompson and I can really identify with Karen's point. We're always being told how we're supposed to act like adults and show respect for our parents—well I think "turn about's fair play." If a parent does something to offend his kid, why shouldn't he apologize? Isn't the kid worth it?
Mr. Kersteen: I think I see your point ... *(Mrs. Kersteen and some of the other parents look at him in shock while the others look on with interest).* But it goes way beyond just apologizing. If we're supposed to treat each other with respect, then that *includes* apologizing, but it also includes a lot of other things. Like explaining why things are the way they are. And including kids in the decision process on something that affects the family. Allowing the kid to be an active part of the family instead of just a passive lump.
Karen: Yeah Dad! We are not babies anymore. You can't just say "because I said so," and expect us to be satisfied. I think we deserve to have things explained to us.
Mrs. Kersteen: What kind of things?
Kristi: Like when you were having trouble on your job, Dad. You were impossible to live with and it seemed like you and

Mom were up all night talking almost every night. Do you know what Karen and I thought was going on? *(Mr. and Mrs. Kersteen shake their heads.)*

Karen: We thought you were getting a divorce!

Kristi: And we were scared to death! You could have saved us all that worry if you had just told us what was going on.

Karen: *And* we would have been able to treat Daddy better because we would have understood why he was so grumpy!

Mrs. Kersteen: I had no idea....

Karen: And Mom, you know that when you are angry and upset, you say things to us that you don't really mean. *(Mrs. Kersteen nods.)* Well, we know you don't mean 'em either, but it sure would be a lot easier to get over them if you would just apologize!

Mr. Kersteen: I uh, well girls, ahhum! That doesn't seem to be too big of a request. I uh, think we could try to do that, don't you, Alice? *(Mrs. Kersteen nods.)* But we will, of course, expect the same courtesy from you! *(The girls grin.)*

Patti: Good! How about you, Dad? Do you think you could treat me with a little more respect?

Mr. Thompson: Respect?! I don't get it. I leave you to fend for yourself and take care of your brother most of the time—isn't that showing that I have confidence in your abilities?

Patti: No, Dad. I don't think you have any choice but to leave me in charge—since Mom left. But if I'm going to have that much responsibility, it would sure help if you'd *talk* to me, tell me what you expect from me.

Mr. Thompson: Patti, I don't know what you mean. Can you be more specific?

Patti: Well, you grounded me last week because I let Jason go to the game with his friends—but you never told me he wasn't supposed to go—how was I to know?

Mr. Thompson: Patti, why didn't you tell me this when I grounded you?

Patti: I *tried,* Dad! You just wouldn't listen! You were so mad—

Mr. Thompson: It's all coming back to me now. I wasn't mad at you, Patti. I'd just found out that I had two days to redo a report that took me a month to prepare. When I got home at 8:30 and found that Jason wasn't there, I guess I let my worry and frustrations explode all over you. *(Pause. Addresses the Kersteen girls):* This must be an example of what *you* were talking about. If I'd explained to Patti why I was so upset ...

Patti: Or just taken a moment to listen to me ...

Mr. Thompson *(sighs):* You're right, Patti, I owe you an apology, and your brother too. And yes, I can see that I need to take you into my confidence more. Things have just been so hard since your mother left—

Patti: For us too, Dad. Jason and I need someone to talk to about it.

Mr. Thompson *(reaches over and lays his hand on Patti's knee):* OK Kid,—I mean—Patti! *(Laughter.)* We'll work on this. I'll schedule time for you and Jason, and we'll try to put some order into our lives.

Patti *(beaming):* That'd be great, Dad!

TJ *(timidly):* Ahhh, I'd like to pick up on that point about explaining things ... *(looks fearfully at his dad).*

Mr. James *(gruffly):* Go ahead.

TJ: Well you two are always telling me how disappointed you are in me—how I don't live up to your expectations. You don't like my hair, my clothes, the way I keep my room, my grades, or my friends.

Mr. James: That about covers it.

TJ: But I don't know what you want! How can I live up to your expectations when I don't know what they are?

Mrs. James: Why Tommy, we've always told you—

TJ: No you haven't! When have you ever told me *before* I do something what it is that you expect to see? You've never told me what kind of clothes you want me to wear, or what the rules are about my room. One week it's OK for me to have my friends over, and the next week it isn't. I can't follow the rules when I don't know what they are!

(Mr. and Mrs. James look at each other rather sheepishly.)

Mr. James: I guess I just see so much of myself in you that I expect you to be able to read my mind.

TJ *(amazed):* You what? You think *I'm* like *you?*

Mr. James: Well sure, Kid. I was just like you when I was your age. I messed around in school and never did what I was supposed to at home. My parents were always yelling at me—*(he breaks off, looks at TJ, and grins.)* Like father, like son, huh?

TJ: Good grief, Dad! I didn't know I was like you!

Mr. James: Well you are. And I want things to be better for you than they were for me—that's why I push you so hard—I want so much for you to excel—*(Mr. James' voice breaks and he clenches his fists on his knees. He looks at his wife for help.)*

Mrs. James: Tommy, what your dad is trying to say—

TJ *(breaks in with wonder in his eyes and voice):* I know, Mom. He means—he means that—he loves me. *(TJ's voice also* breaks and he lowers his head. There is silence for a moment and several people in the group wipe their eyes. After a moment, Mr. Witter speaks.)

Mr. Witter *(clears his throat):* Nobody appointed me group leader here, but if nobody minds, I'd like to say a few words. *(Everybody nods, says "Go ahead," "Sure," etc.)* I'd just like to point out that this group never even got past the first question on this list, yet it seems obvious to me that we've broken through several barriers. *(Others nod and agree.)* Imagine what might be accomplished if each family made time to discuss one question a day—or even one a week! I agree wholeheartedly with Simon and Ross; we're here tonight because we love our children *(looks at Rob)* whether we actually fathered them or not. I can tell just from this brief time with you tonight that there isn't a parent here who wouldn't give life or limb to save the life of one of you kids. If Simon and Ross are right, and I believe they are, all we need to do to protect our children from the threat of suicide is build their self-esteem, and we do that by expressing our unconditional love. Well, I see that Simon and Ross are about to call for our attention, so I'd just like to thank God for such a program, and ask that He be with each one of us as we try to put these things into practice.

(The group nods and murmurs and expresses their appreciation.)
Ross *(from up front):* Well, what do you think everybody? Was tonight worthwhile?
(Kids cheer and whistle, adults laugh and applaud as the lights go down.)

END OF SCENE 1

SCENE 2

As the lights dim on scene one, the players move off the stage. Patti and her dad stand, put on their coats, and move toward the front edge of the stage. A spotlight comes on them.

Mr. Thompson: Patti—
Patti: I know, Dad. You're mad at me for saying what I did, aren't you?
Mr. Thompson: No, no I'm not mad. You kinda put me on the spot, but you were just being honest. I guess I deserved it.
Patti *(surprised):* Grief, Dad! These guys must have gotten to you!
Mr. Thompson *(laughs a little):* Yeah, I guess they did. And *that's* why I want to talk to you. And if I don't do it now, I'll probably never get up the courage again.
Patti: Dad, what is it? You're scaring me!
Mr. Thompson *(puts his arm around Patti so that they are both facing the audience. He looks down at the ground):* I don't mean to scare you ... but this rap session tonight started some pretty serious thinking on my part. *(Pause.)* You know, *(another pause)* your mother left me because she said I was cold. She said I stopped loving her years ago. *(He takes his arm away from Patti and shoves both hands into pockets. He turns toward Patti.)* Honey, that isn't true—I *never* stopped loving your mom. But, I stopped telling her that I loved her, and I stopped treating her like I loved her, so what else was she supposed to believe?
Patti *(fighting tears):* Dad, I don't know what I'm supposed to say....
Mr. Thompson: Nothing, Honey. Just listen. *(He rakes his hand over his head in a gesture of frustration.)* When your mother first accused me of being cold, I just laughed at her. *(Patti shakes her head.)* I guess I was just too caught up in my work, and I *never* thought she'd leave me! I just wrote it off as midlife crisis or something. Anyway, any chance we had of working things out got slimmer and slimmer as the months rolled by—I just never *listened* to her! *(Suddenly, he takes Patti's hand and leads her over to two of the closest chairs. The spotlight follows. Mr. Thompson moves a chair around till it's facing another, he and Patti sit down and he takes both her hands into both of his.)* Patti, what I'm trying to tell you is that Simon and Ross are right about more than just kids and parents; communication, and expressions of love, are the key to *every* relationship, and I really fouled up with your mother! I know

you and your brother are bitter about her leaving with another man, but Patti, I practically drove her to that! And now, tonight, it has suddenly dawned on me that I could be in danger of losing you kids, too.

Patti: Aw Dad, we're too young to leave.

Mr. Thompson: But not for long! Patti, you'll be eighteen in only _____ years! Besides, I'm not worried so much about losing you physically as I am about losing you emotionally. *(Grips her hands tighter and leans forward in earnest.)* Patti, I love you! And I love Jason and if anything happen to either of you—*(He breaks off and shakes his head. Patti hugs him—she can move to a chair alongside him or they can stand—but they are both crying. After a moment, they part, grope for tissues, wipe their eyes, sniff, etc.)*

Patti: Dad, none of us have been exactly easy to get along with since Mom left. Maybe we've all been scared that someone else would leave. *(Pause.)* I don't think I knew that was what was bothering me until right now—but hearing you say that you love me and don't ever want to lose me makes me feel *so* much better—kinda relieved like. *(They grin at each other and hug again. Patti continues, rather shyly:)* I bet Jason would like to know for sure too.

Mr. Thompson *(claps his arm around Patti's shoulders and they head out):* And I intend to tell him just as soon as we get home! Come on, let's go!

CURTAIN

DISCUSSION QUESTIONS

1. At the beginning of the play, Karen wondered if kids could influence their parents personalities. She suggested that Rob had a neat dad because he was a neat kid, and that her own dad was about "half wonderful" because he had one optimistic daughter and one pessimistic daughter. What do you think about that theory? Even if kids learn personality traits from their parents in the first place, do you think they can later change the way their parents have always done things?

2. When Rob told his friends that neither of his parents had ever said "I love you" to him, Kristi asked him if he had ever said it to them. Do you think that was a fair question? Should kids be the ones to break a barrier like that? Rob suggested that some parents aren't comfortable with expressions of love because they grew up without them. Is that a good explanation? Is it a good reason to let things continue that way? Do parents or kids have more responsibility to try and make things better? Or, is it a question of responsibility?

3. In the past, men were told that expressing any kind of tender emotion (love, sadness, even happiness sometimes) was not "manly" so men learned to hide their feelings. What do you think about that? Are men still told that? Is there such a thing as "masculine emotion" and "feminine emotion" or do we all feel the same things? What about Jesus—did He express His love freely and openly? Did it affect the way He was thought of by those around Him?

4. Do expressions of love invite expressions of love in return? When you're around a cheerful person do you begin to feel cheerful? When you're around a griper, do you feel like griping too? People do have a great influence on each other. How can we use this fact to make our own lives better?

5. As the kids were talking, Kristi told Dave that she would pray for him and Rob said that it was God's will for families to have good communication. Have you ever heard anybody talk so easily about God to their school friends? What do you think would happen if you told a non-Christian friend that you would pray for him? What did Dave do? Do you think that many Christians *assume* that non-Christians do not want to hear about God? Is this necessarily true?

6. How many of the keys to communication do you remember from the acronym "GET REAL"? Since you first heard these tips, have you tried to use them? If so, what were the results? Would you be willing to take a list of these tips home and share them with your parents?

7. Why do you think it is difficult for some people to express their love? If you ever run into that problem, do you think you'll be able to offer some advice?

GENTLEMEN PREFER LADIES
(and vice versa)

CAST OF CHARACTERS
Melissa—junior-high or high-school girl
Melissa's mother
Melissa's baby brother
Amy—high-school girl
Amy's mother
Mr./Ms. Thompson—teacher (man or woman)
Jackson—high school student
Jeff—high-school student
Tony—high-school student
Sylvia—high-school student
Andrea—high-school student
Pete—high-school student
Kim—high-school student
Renee—high-school student
Brad—high-school student
Mike—high-school student
Two middle-aged women shoppers
Glen—youth-group sponsor
Shirley—youth-group sponsor
Todd—youth-group sponsor

SCENES
Act 1 Scene 1: Amy's kitchen
          2: Thompson's classroom
          3: McDonald's
Act 2 Scene 1: Amy's living room
          2: Thompson's classroom
          3: Youth-group room at church

ACT 1 SCENE 1

Typical kitchen, typical house. Mother is dressed for work, breakfast dishes and cooking utensils are piled by sink, cereal boxes and carton of milk, bottle of juice, box of doughnuts, bowls, etc. are still on kitchen table. Preschool-age child is playing on the floor (or you could use a doll, wrapped in a car seat/carrier). Mother is obviously distraught as she glances at watch.

Mother: Melissa! This is absolutely the last time I'm going to call you! If you're not ready to leave in two minutes, you can walk to school! It's a quarter to eight, I still have to drop Joey off at the daycare center, and—

Melissa *(comes sauntering in dressed as much like Madonna or Cyndi Lauper as you feel appropriate):* All right! All right, Mom! Keep your suit on! I'm ready. *(She pours herself a glass of juice and drinks it during the following conversation.)*

Mother: Ready? In that outfit? You look like a cheap hobo! You *know* what your father said about wearing those sleazy clothes to school!

Melissa: Aw, Mom, give me a break, will you? All you ever do is hassle me about my clothes! Anyway, today is "Rock Day" at school and everybody will be dressed like Rockers.

Mother: Rock Day? I don't remember any such day! Why don't I ever hear of these things in advance? Did they send a notice home with you? How do I know you're telling me the truth?

Melissa *(slams juice glass down on the table):* Well, just thanks a lot Mom! Thank you for calling me a liar!

Mother: Melissa, honey, that's not what I meant—it's just that we've been through this so many times before and you've tried everything to get your own way. . . . Your father and I know it's important for you to dress like your friends. We try to go along as much as possible, but Melissia, this is just going too far. . . . *(Glances at watch again.)* Look, I am already late for work so I'll wait for you while you run up and change.

Melissa: Don't do me any big favors! Just go! Go on and go to your stupid job and take that stupid baby with you! I'll go put on the stupid, ugly clothes that you and daddy allow, and I'll be the *only* kid at school today dressed like a wimp. *Everybody* will laugh at me, but what do you care? *(She continues her tantrum as she stomps off. Yelling and stomping is heard offstage.)* Just ruin my day, ruin my life! Just let everyone at school make fun of me because you and dad have "standards!"

(Mother stands in center of kitchen, shoulders drooping. She

looks at her watch again, then goes and picks up her purse, briefcase, and the baby.)

Mother (calling): Melissa? Melissa, honey? *(No answer.)* Melissa, please don't forget to lock the door, OK? *(No answer.)* And I've left your lunch money right here on the table, OK? *(She listens a moment for an answer, sighs again, and leaves, saying softly to herself)* Have a good day, Melissa.

(After a silent moment or two, Melissa pokes her head into the kitchen.)

Melissa: Good! She's finally gone! *(She comes into view wearing an unbuttoned shirt over her Madonna clothes tied in a knot over her midriff. She has taken off some of the jewelry. She adjusts the shirt.)* This is better anyway. This way I can take it off, or wear it long and have a couple of different looks today! *(She grabs a doughnut from the box, stuffs the money in her pocket, and runs out, slamming the door.)*

END OF SCENE 1

ACT 1 SCENE 2

School classroom before class. Kids are dressed in several ways—a couple of well-dressed, nice-looking preppy outfits, a couple of nerds in old-fashioned clothes, most are wearing rock-star fashions, punk outfits, the Madonna look, etc.—a typical collection.

Melissa is talking to her best friend, Amy, by the door. Amy is wearing the full "Madonna" regalia. Other kids are clustered in groups, one or two are sleeping. The nerds are alone, uncomfortable, and self-conscious. The part of the teacher can be played by either man or a woman.

Amy: I like that shirt Melissa. It looks really sexy like that! But how come your old lady let you wear those clothes to school?

Melissa: She didn't "let" me! I left after she did and will get home before she does, so I'll just change. But I had to go through the same old hassle before she left. *(Mimics.)* "In that outfit? You look like a cheap hobo!"

Amy: Hobo? *Hobo?* What's a hobo? *(Both laugh uproariously.)*

Melissa: I know, my mom's in the Middle Ages. I guess she didn't want to call me a tramp, but she might as well. Dad does.

Amy: Yeah, your old man is something else. I'm sure glad he's not *my* dad.

Melissa: Well, he's not so bad most of the time, but he's got this thing about the way I dress—it's an obsession with him.

Amy: Yeah, I know. Look, I gotta go or I'm gonna be late. I'll meet you after third period by the door, OK? *(Melissa nods.)* Can you go to McDonald's for lunch?

Melissa: Sure, I've got money. *(Bell rings. Amy bolts for the door, groups break up, and the kids start to drift toward chairs. Melissa calls after Amy.)* See ya after third!

(As Melissa starts for her desk, she bumps into Jackson's desk. He's one of the well-dressed, preppy types.)

Melissa: Hey! Watch where you're going!

Jackson *(kindly):* Well really, Melissa, I wasn't *going* anywhere. *(Some of the other kids snicker.)*

Melissa *(angry and embarrassed):* Well, you shouldn't have your stupid desk sitting right in the middle of where I'm walking! Creep!

(Jackson starts to reply but is cut off by a loud voice from the back of the room where a group of punk dressers are gathered. Tony is one of the wildest-dressed).

Tony: Hey Melissa! Quit messin' with Jackson and get on back here. *(Other kids laugh out loud.)*

Melissa: I ain't messin' with him! *(Fakes a punch at Jackson who throws up his arm to protect himself.)* You wimp! Why don't you stay outta my life?

(Jackson hangs his head, most of the other kids laugh, a few shake their heads at Melissa's behavior. Just then the teacher walks in.)

Mr./Ms. Thompson: OK, what's going on in here? Looks like you're at the center of it, Melissa, again.

Melissa: I'm not doing anything! Jackson's pickin' on me.

Thompson: Oh, I'm sure. *(Kids laugh.)* All right everybody, please take your seats. Let's get this show on the road.

(As everybody begins to settle down, the teacher pulls a literature book out of his/her briefcase and opens it up.)

Thompson: We left off yesterday in the middle of a discussion on the poetry form called "haiku." Who remembers what country developed this type of poem? *(Several hands go up.)* Jeff?

Jeff: Japan?

Thompson: Right. Sylvia, what is so unusual about this form?

Sylvia: Well, it's really short.

Thompson: Yes, how short is it?

Melissa and Tony *(snicker from the back and say in unison):* It is so short ... *(Class laughs, but looks for the teacher's reaction.)*

Thompson: Very funny, you two. Now, one of you can tell me, just how short is a haiku? Tony? *(Silence.)* Melissa?

Melissa *(after a short pause)*: Well, I think it's only three lines long.
Thompson: Very good! *(Tony and several others give looks of fake admiration.)* Three lines composed of how many syllables? Anyone? *(Several hands go up, including Jackson's.)* Jackson?
Jackson: The first line of a haiku is five syllables long the second, seven syllables, and the last is five, for a total of seventeen syllables.
(Before the teacher can respond, the class troublemakers in the back go crazy. They mimic Jackson in fake admiration as before.)
Thompson *(exasperated)*: Look! What is it with you people today? You're even more obnoxious than usual. Now settle down before I start assigning penalties. *(Sighs.)* Jackson, that is absolutely correct. Now, there is one more very important defining factor of a haiku. Does anyone remember what it is?
(A couple of kids raise their hands rather tentatively. Teacher calls on Andrea, a well-dressed preppy type.)
Thompson: Yes, Andrea?
Andrea: Well, I think you said yesterday that the first two lines set up a mood or scene and the last line challenges it or changes it, or something.
Thompson: Exactly right! Very good, Andrea. *(Melissa and Tony and group start to mock. Thompson silences them with a look.)* Now, you have several examples of Japanese haiku in your book on page ... *(checks his/her own book)* page 232. I want you to study those and then see if you can come up with one of your own. *(Class groans.)* Oh now, come on! It's only three lines, seventeen syllables. Surely each of you is capable of that!
(The class has been finding the correct page in their books, shuffling notebooks, getting out pen and paper as Thompson speaks. Now they begin to settle down, reading the examples and thinking. As soon as it gets really quiet, Tony flicks Melissa with his pencil.)
Melissa *(loud, angry whisper)*: Ouch! Whaddaya want?
Tony: Ya got one yet?
Melissa: Well, give me a minute!
Thompson: Tony, Melissa, this is not a joint project. Please pipe down.
(Melissa gives Tony a scathing look and goes back to thinking and scribbling in her notebook. All over the room, kids are counting syllables, ticking them off their fingers, scratching out, shaking heads, trying again. Thompson walks around the room stopping

to read papers, giving encouragement. When s/he reaches Pete s/he stops.)

Thompson: Pete, I like this. Would you read it to the class, please?

Pete (embarrassed, he stands up):
>A picnic is planned,
>>Friends will come from far away.
>
>Rain is predicted.

(Class murmurs appreciation. Melissa and Tony make faces at each other.)

Thompson: See how he's created a mood of eager anticipation with the first two lines, and then spoils it with the third? (Class nods.) Very good, Pete. Anyone else?

(Kim, one of the quiet girls who is obviously not apart of the fashion scene, shyly raises her hand.)

Thompson: Yes, Kim, go ahead.

Kim (stands):
>Today is the day
>>When my dreams are realized.
>
>Why am I so sad?

Thompson (excited): I really like that! (Ticks the syllables off on his fingers as he repeats the poem.)
>To-day is the day
>>When my dreams are re-a-lized
>
>Why am I so sad?

Very good, Kim! (To rest of class.) Kim has created a mood, a thought process that goes even deeper than Pete's. But don't take offense Pete, because yours is very good too. Who can explain what I mean? (A couple of hands go up.) Renee?

Renee: Well, do you mean, like, we knew that Pete's picnic was going to be ruined because of rain, but we sorta are left to wonder why Kim is sad? I mean, if all her dreams are going to come true?

Thompson: Exactly! And even deeper than that! It leads us to wonder if she's sad *because* her dreams have all been realized, because she has nothing left to dream for. (Pauses.) Very good poetry, Kim.

(Ever since Pete read his haiku, Melissa, Tony, and crew have been getting increasingly rowdy. Now Thompson falls silent and stands at the front of the room staring at them. When they finally catch on and settle down, s/he speaks.)

Thompson: Just what do you find so amusing back there? (A couple of them snicker.) Perhaps you have a haiku to share with the class? (Tony snickers again and punches Melissa. She

brushes him off and sits primly, looking at Thompson.) Tony?
Tony *(belligerent)*: What?
Thompson: Do you have a haiku?
Tony: No I don't, but Brad does! *(Melissa, Brad, and several others gasp and stare in shock at Tony.)*
Thompson: Well, please read it for us, Brad, we're all waiting.
Brad: Uh, well, uh, I didn't write it.
Thompson: No? Who did? *(No answer.)* I see. Well, perhaps I'd better read this haiku.
(Teacher walks back to Brad's desk, pulls a rumpled piece of paper out from under his arm, and reads it. There is not a sound in the room. Thompson lowers the paper and speaks quietly.)
Thompson: This is trash. *(Starts toward the front of the room still holding the paper.)* This is so juvenile. And such a waste of a good mind! *(Melissa looks up in surprise.)* Whoever wrote this, this drivil, obviously has a good grasp of the poetry form. The meter is right, the element of surprise is right, but what a waste of talent and what a waste of my time and the time of those who are in this class to learn something! *(Faces the rowdies.)* I don't really care which one of you wrote this garbage. Together you've disturbed every class since the year began, so I'm putting you all on probation. *(Outcries of protest from the bunch, Brad is the loudest.)* Oh, Brad, you don't think that's fair?
Brad *(grumbles)*: I told ya, man, I didn't write it!
Thompson: Do you care to tell me who did? *(Brad shakes his head "no.")* Tony? *(Shakes his head "no.")* Kim? *(Same reaction. Melissa has been staring at her desk top all this time.)* I'll say this much for you; you're a loyal bunch. That's admirable, but in this situation, you're all going down together. I'm putting you all on probation until you demonstrate to me that you're ready to grow up and start acting like the young ladies and gentlemen that you should be instead of a bunch of immature, low-class, gutter-brains. *(Bell rings.)* Well! That ends another almost completely wasted hour. My apologies to those of you who were enjoying the study of haiku, and who had hoped to learn something today. Your assignment for tomorrow is to finish reading chapter fourteen, and everyone, *(pauses,)* everyone will turn in an acceptable haiku tomorrow. Extra points for those who write more than one. Class dismissed.
(The kids make a racket gathering up their things and heading out. Melissa's bunch is strangely quiet. Brad heads over to her.)
Brad: Look you, I'm not taking the rap for your stupid poem!

My old man's gonna skin me alive if I come home on probation!

Tony: Listen to this! You didn't seem to mind reading it, did you? Thought it was pretty funny before we got into trouble, didn't you?

Brad: Yeah, well, if *you* hadn't opened your big mouth—

Tony: Oh yeah? It's always everybody else's fault, isn't it?

(Brad starts to get physical but Melissa interrupts.)

Melissa: Hey! Save it, you two! I'll tell Thompson that I'm the one who wrote it, but s/he said s/he didn't care. Said s/he was putting us on probation because we've been messing around all year, so I don't think you've got much to blame on me!

(The others reluctantly agree as they all grumble their way out the door. Melissa is last in the group and just as she is at the door, Jackson, who has been sitting at this desk and is the only other person in the room, calls out to her.)

Jackson: Hey, Melissa!

Melissa: What?

Jackson: I'm sorry you got into trouble.

Melissa: Oh I'm sure! You just want to rub it in don'tcha? Cuz I made fun of you?

Jackson: No Melissa! I know you didn't mean what you said to me. I mean, I know you only do those things to get attention. *(Melissa looks surprised and Jackson is flustered.)* Well, look, I just mean to say that I wish you didn't feel like you have to act like that.

Melissa: Act like what? Look buddy, I ain't doing nothin for attention—this is *me*, this is the way I am!

Jackson *(grins)*: Well I hope not. I hope it's just a stage!

Melissa: What are you talking about?

Jackson: Well, look, you and I have been in school and church together since we were little kids and I just happen to like the old Melissa a little better, and well, you know, I kinda wish you hadn't changed.

Melissa: Who cares what you think or what you like? You sound like my old man! *(Turns and stomps out of the room.)* Grief! I don't believe this!

(Jackson stands alone in the room, disheartened, looking after Melissa, as lights go down.)

END OF SCENE 2

ACT 1 SCENE 3

McDonald's at lunchtime. Set up a counter where kids can order and receive their food. You might want to save some burger boxes and bags from McDonald's, or just go buy a bunch of food before the play. Set up rows of small tables and chairs to look like the booths and tables in McDonald's.

Kids are all over the place—yelling to each other, throwing french fries, being a general nuisance. A couple of middle-aged women with shopping bags are at a center table in the front and seem to be trapped there. They are shocked at much of the activity around them. Tony, Brad, and some other boys are at a table next to the women when Melissa and Amy come in.

Tony *(hollers across the room to Melissa as she comes in)*: Yo! Melissa! *(Melissa and Amy laugh and wave to the boys.)*
Melissa: Be right there Tony! *(She and Amy get in line.)*
Brad: Did you guys hear about what happened in Thompson's class this morning?
Jeff: I heard you two got put on probation.
Brad: Yeah. Melissa wrote this really raunchy poem and Thompson got ahold of it.
Mike: So s/he punished all of you?
Tony: Yeah, well, we *were* all goofing off. *(Brad agrees.)*
Jeff: So what about the poem? What'd she write, anyway?
(Tony and Brad look at each other and laugh, Brad leans over and says something in a low voice to the others. When he finishes, they all howl with exaggerated laughter.)
Mike: Oh wow! That Melissa's really something! I didn't know she had it in her!
Tony *(very knowingly)*: Yeah, she's just full of talent!
(All the boys laugh raucously as Melissa and Amy make their way over to the table, carrying trays.)
Amy: What's so funny?
Brad: Oh, we were just reciting Melissa's *wonderful* poem.
Amy: Yeah, I heard about that!
Melissa *(milking the moment, says suggestively)*: Oh yes, writing hot poetry is just one of my many talents! *(The boys howl.)*
Tony *(yells)*: That's what I just told 'em!
Melissa: Oh yeah, Tony? Well, what I'd like to know is, how would you know?
(All the kids scream with laughter. the boys shift around to make room for the girls. The two women have heard all of this and now one of them speaks.)

Lady 1: And I thought *my* kids were bad!
Lady 2: I know. I just don't understand kids today. Would your daughter ever have dreamed of going out in public dressed like *that!*
Lady 1: Never! And if she had, there's no way I would have allowed it. And did you hear the way that girl talked? What kind of a mother does she have?
Melissa *(embarrassed and defensive, jumps up from her place and stands between the women and her group):* There's nothing wrong with my mother! She told me not to wear this! *(Realizes what she has said and assumes a defiant air.)* She's just as old-fashioned as you are! And that's why I don't pay any attention to her!
Tony: Way to go, Mel!
Amy: Yeah, you tell 'em!
Lady 2 *(kindly):* Dear, don't you think your mother has your best interest at heart? Don't you realize that she's trying to protect you?
Melissa *(angry):* I'm not your "dear." *(Confused.)* Whaddaya mean, "protect me?" Protect me from what? I'm not in any danger.
Lady 1: Well, perhaps not from these boys ... *(looks them over).* If they are your friends and you trust them, maybe they would never harm you. But if you go around dressed like that, you're just asking for trouble.
Melissa *(really embarrassed):* Hey lady, why don't you mind your own business? Nobody asked for your opinion! *(Stomps back to her place at the table.)* Silly old bats! Sound just like my mother! *(Mimics.)* "You're just asking for trouble."
Amy: Oh, just ignore them, Mel. All old people are alike.
Brad: Yeah, always lookin' for trouble.
Mike: Whaddaya mean?
Brad: You know, always think the worst of people. Just because they don't like the clothes we wear, they think we're no good.
Tony: Yeah, but "you can't tell a book by its cover!"
(Everyone laughs except Melissa. The ladies have finished their lunch and are now leaving. Melissa looks after them.)
Amy: Why so glum, chum?
Melissa *(looks down at herself and wraps her shirt closer around her):* Oh, I was just thinking ... what *do* you guys think of the way I dress?
Mike: Are you serious? *(Sees by Melissa's face that she is.)* Oh. Well, I think you look pretty sexy, right guys? *(They all agree.)*
Brad: But you don't dress any more trashy than any of the rest

of the girls. Besides, we all know what kind of girl you *really* are—underneath all that make-up! *(Laughs nervously.)*
Melissa *(wounded):* Do you think I wear too much make-up?
Tony *(to Brad):* Smart move! *(To Melissa.)* Well, not exactly—
Melissa: What do you mean, "not exactly"?
Tony: Well hey! Lighten up, will ya?
Melissa: No. This is serious. I want to know if you think I wear too much make-up. *(To Brad.)* And I want to know what you mean by "knowing the kind of girl I really am." *(The boys are uncomfortable.)*
Tony: I just mean that *some* people might think that you wear too much make-up, but I don't. I know that it's just the fashion started by Madonna and Cyndi Lauper. And that it's really just for fun to look like a . . . um, to wear a lot of make-up.
Brad: Yeah, and just because you dress like a . . . you know, dress for flash, that doesn't mean that you're actually a trampy person and we all know you're not.
Tony, Rick, Jeff: That's right!
(Melissa looks at Amy, who returns her look with a shrug.)
Melissa: And when I talk and act trampy, you know I'm only kidding?
Boys: Well yeah, sure, of course.
Melissa *(lightening up):* Well, that's great! Now I've only got to worry about everybody who doesn't know me!
(Everybody laughs and hurries up to finish lunch as the lights go down.)

END OF ACT 1

ACT 2, SCENE 1

Amy's living room. She's still in her school clothes, sprawled on the couch, talking on the phone.
Amy: Yeah, it was weird. The guys were trying to be nice, but we could tell that they really *do* think we wear too much make-up. *(Pauses.)* No, I never would have guessed it either, but who ever knows what guys are thinking? *(Pauses.)* I don't know. What would you do? Melissa is really upset about it. She told me on the way home that she feels like she's been lied to and used. *(Pause.)* Because! She thought the guys liked it! She said she never had any idea that they thought the Madonna look was trampy—well, neither of us did! I always thought it was just for fun, but I sure don't like the idea of guys talking about me behind my back!
(Amy's mother comes in from stage left carrying purse, briefcase, and full grocery bag. As she passes Amy she speaks.)

Mother: Will you help me carry in the groceries, please?
Amy *(to phone)*: What? Oh yeah, my mom came in. Listen, I gotta help unload the groceries. I'll call ya later, OK? *(Pauses.)* OK. See ya. *(She hangs up the phone and starts toward the door yelling back over her shoulder.)* Wait till I tell you what happened today, Mom. You're gonna die! *(She goes out the door and her mother reenters from the way she exited, wiping her hands on a towel.)*
Mother *(quietly)*: And wait till I tell you who almost *did* die.
(Amy comes in, struggling under two grocery bags.)
Amy: Whew! No wonder food puts weight on you! *(Passes her mother and yells from offstage.)* Did you talk to Melissa's mom yet? Did she tell you what happened today?
Mother: No, I didn't. But I talked to Janice's mom. *(Amy reenters the living room.)*
Amy: Janice? Hey! I don't think she was in school today. Is she sick? Come on, let's put this stuff away. *(Gestures toward kitchen.)*
Mother: In a minute, Dear. *(Amy looks puzzled.)* Come on in here and sit down. I need to talk to you.
Amy *(defensively)*: Oh! So you *did* hear about what happened today.
Mother: No, I didn't. Is it very important?
Amy *(lightly)*: No, not at all! It can wait. What do you want to talk to me about?
(Mother moves over to couch sits down and pats the seat next to her.)
Mother: Come and sit down, Amy.
Amy *(nervous, goes and sits)*: Mom! What is it? You're scaring me! Did something happen to Daddy?
Mother *(takes one of Amy's hands and holds it with both of hers)*: No, Amy, your dad and your brothers are fine, but something terrible has happened to Janice. I ran into Mrs. Johnson at the supermarket and she told me that last night Janice was coming home through the park, by herself, and a gang of boys stopped her. She knew the boys, and she thought they were only fooling around, teasing her, trying to scare her. But when she did get scared, and tried to get away—oh Amy! I'm so sorry! Janice was raped and beaten up very badly. *(Amy is stunned. She doesn't respond, only reaches for her mother's hands with her other hand. Her mother continues.)* It seems that they'd been drinking. They called Janice a "tease" and told her it was time to pay up. I guess she was playing along with them until she realized they were drunk.

Amy: I'm not going to listen to anymore of this! Janice is my friend! How can you use this as an excuse to lecture me? *(Her mother starts to answer but Amy throws up her hands in a "stop" motion as she storms out of the room.)* I'm not going to listen to one more word!
(Mother's arms drop to her sides and her shoulders slump. Her back is nearly to the audience as she speaks.)
Mother: Oh Amy, Amy. How can I make you understand?
END OF SCENE 1

ACT 2 SCENE 2
Thompson's classroom. All the students are in their seats and there is no boisterous laughing or talking going on. Melissa is dressed in a more subdued manner, but still not what you'd call modest.

Melissa: I can't believe it happened! I almost went shopping with Janice—I would have been *with* her coming home!
Brad: You?! *I* was supposed to be with Rod and those other guys! The only reason I wasn't was because Dad grounded me because of the probation I got here!
Melissa *(in awe):* What would you have done, Brad? Would you have ... done it, too?
Brad *(angry):* Of course not! That's crazy! It's all crazy! I don't know what happened and I don't know what got into those guys!
Tony: Of course, they were all pretty smashed—
Melissa *(turns on him):* Do you think that's some kind of excuse?
Tony *(sheepishly):* No ... but if a guy's been drinking and a girl like Janice comes along—
Melissa: Just *what* do you mean, "a girl like Janice"? And you'd better be careful of what you say because she's my friend!
Brad: She's my friend, too, or at least she was ... but Mel, you know what Tony means. She's a fox, and she's stacked, and she dresses to call attention to both those facts!
Melissa *(shouting):* You both make me sick! Just because a girl is pretty, and wears pretty clothes, you think she's asking to be raped? Talk about a double standard! You talk about what a "fox" some girl is, and you like it when she wears sexy clothes, and then you turn around and blame her for getting raped!
(During this tirade, Thompson has entered the room. Everyone

but Melissa saw him/her come in. *Now, when no one responds to Melissa, she turns and sees him/her too, and slumps into her seat.)*
Thompson: No, I'm not going to yell at you, Melissa. We're all wound up pretty tight around here. You raised some good questions in your little speech there, and I surely wish I had some answers. You kids need to think about not only what Janice is going through, but what those boys are going through. *(The girls start to protest.)* No, wait a minute. You all know those guys. They're not the scum of the earth. They were drinking and things got out of hand. Do you think they *planned* to hurt Janice, or anyone else? Now they face prison sentences and will carry the title of "rapist" for the rest of their lives. It's a tragedy any way you look at it. *(The room is silent.)* Well, I know you need some time to sort this out and you need to talk it over with someone. Unfortunately, the school administration has asked us to conduct business as usual. *(More protests from the class. Thompson holds up his/her hands.)* I know, I know. Haiku and other poetry forms are the furthest things from your minds. But actually, I'm afraid I don't have any answers for you anyway. I wish I did. *(Jackson raises his hand rather timidly.)* Yes, Jackson, what is it?
Jackson *(hesitantly):* Well, Sir, some of us go to the same church and are, uh, members of the same youth group. We've been studying a series of personal characteristics of a Christian and this Sunday night we're going to talk about modesty. I thought that maybe, in light of the controversy surrounding what's happened to Janice, um, maybe some of the other kids in this class would like to come, because maybe we'll find some answers there.
Thompson: Sure Jackson, couldn't hurt. Well, I don't know what the school board would have to say about my repeating that invitation, so if any of you are interested, see Jackson after class. Now, let's try to get our minds on the business at hand. *(Lights begin to fade, Thompson's voice gets small.)* Turn to page 234 in your literature books. . . .
END OF SCENE 2

ACT 2 SCENE 3
Sunday night, in the youth room of the church. Every kid in the play is there plus a few new ones. The room is packed. They are quiet, but animated conversations are going on all over the room. Battle lines appear to be drawn, with angry girls on one

side of the room, and defiant boys on the other. Several adult sponsors (Glen, Shirley, and Todd) appear nervous.

Glen *(steps into middle of room):* Well, ahhum, *(false cheerfulness)* welcome to all our visitors! *(His welcome falls flat and his shoulders fall.)* I guess it's no secret why you're all here. Janice *is* a member of this group and we're all very much aware of what's happened to her. I understand that you're all here because you want some answers, some explanations. *(Pauses.)* That's a tall order, but we'll do our best. We'll look to the Bible for our answers, and I'll say, just as a word of explanation to our visitors, that the Bible *is* our answer book for life—sort of like an owner's manual. Since the Bible is God's Word, and we are God's creation, we look to the Bible for the answers to life's problems. And, we don't argue with it even if we don't understand, or can't appreciate God's point of view. I guess that'll be the only ground rule for tonight's discussion, OK? Now, before we start, I've asked Shirley to lead us in prayer.

(They all bow their heads as Shirley comes to stand in the center of the room.)

Shirley: Dear Heavenly Father, please help us to come to grips with what has happened. We know there is evil in this world, but we're shocked and hurt that it has come to one so young, and one whom we care so much about. We're also shocked that our friends were the ones to conduct this evil thing. Help us to understand why it happened, and how we can protect ourselves from ever becoming involved in such a crime in any way. Please be with Janice tonight and help her mind and her body to heal. Please be with the boys and their families as they face the charges. And Father, please be with us as we search for some answers. In the name of Your precious Son, Jesus, amen.

(Several others also say, "Amen.")

Todd: I understand that some of you visitors are here tonight because you question what personal modesty has to do with rape. Let me first say that modesty does not have to do *only* with women, and how they dress. Modesty is a way of living, a frame of mind that pertains to both sexes. And let me be *perfectly* clear in saying that I do not blame Janice for what happened to her, and I think I speak for the majority of adults in the church when I say that. The boys who did this are 100 percent responsible for their actions, and the consequences. And rape, in any situation, for any reason, is 100 percent, totally, and absolutely wrong.

Shirley *(speaks from a sitting position within the group)* For the purpose of our discussion, it might help to know that rape is usually, but not always, an act of anger, not an act of lust. Amy came to me before the meeting and said that her mom told her that three fourths of all rape victims are raped by men they know. That is correct. That is why we hear so much about "date rapes" and wives who bring charges against their husbands. If it is usually an act of anger, we need to find out why men are angry and why they feel that rape is an acceptable outlet for that anger.

Glen: It will also help to look at the factors of our society that promote or condone rape—and there are many. You all have grown up in a society that is very, very different from the society your parents and grandparents grew up in, and the new, "enlightened" environment has not always been an advantage for you. The "revolutions" that brought new freedoms also brought new responsibilities, new pressures, and new consequences into our lives—can anyone think of an example of what I am talking about?

Kim: Do you mean like the sexual revolution?

Glen: Yes, that happened way back in the 60's—before most of you were born—so you've had to grow up with the so-called sexual freedom. What are some of the consequences of this freedom?

Pete: More babies! *(Kids chuckle.)*

Glen: Absolutely! And because of the more babies?

Sylvia: More abortions, more unwed mothers, more mothers and children on welfare...

Glen: Yes, and because of that, more child abuse. There's a very delicate relationship between high sexual standards and a high regard for life in general. Andrea, what do I mean by that?

Andrea: Do you mean that as our society became more casual about sex, it also became more casual about abortion and child abuse?

Glen: It would seem that way. But not only less respect for children, but also for...

Melissa: Women?

Glen: Yes, *and* men! I think the sexual revolution caused men to have less respect for women, women to have less respect for men, and everyone to have less respect for themselves.

Shirley: The amazing truth is that people of the world thought they were "liberating" themselves by rejecting God's standards, when they were actually enslaving themselves to a

71

much harsher set of rules. The rules of sexual "freedom" are, flaunt your sexuality, sleep with anyone who turns you on, use whomever you must to make yourself feel "good," but you'll pay the penalty of increased feelings of rejection and loneliness, decreased self-respect, increased risk of veneral disease, unwanted pregnancies, extra-marital affairs, and failed marriages, and ultimately, separation from God. Does this sound like a life-style really worth striving for?

Kids *(shake heads):* No, no way, of course not, etc.

Shirley: But! God's standard of sexual purity until marriage, which the world has tried so hard to get away from, provides a fail-safe protection from most of these risks, and provides a permanent relationship in which two people can enjoy their sexual relationship to the fullest, as God meant it to be. And, God's standard of marriage also provides the security and support—emotional, financial, physical—needed to create a home, a place for children to be born into and raised. But all of this is a much larger discussion than we can get into tonight. Let's get back to naming the ways, as Glen suggested, that casual treatment of sex leads to casual treatment of people. *(Pause.)* Anyone?

Brad: Well, you can't have sex without a partner, and I guess if you're more interested in having sex than you are in the person who is your partner, you can't be treating that person very well, or caring very much about her.

Todd: Exactly! One hundred percent! Give that man a gold star! *(Laughter.)* And, take that one step further; if you choose to believe that you have a right to have sex—no matter what—what right have you taken away from the other person?

Brad: The right to say, "no"?

Todd: One hundred percent right again! Now we are one step further from respecting people and one step closer to rape. Who or what tells us that we have the right to freely express our sexuality and our sexual desires?

(There is a short pause and then a clamor as all the kids speak almost at once—in very rapid succession.)

Amy: Magazine articles! **Pete:** Song lyrics!
Melissa: Movie stars! **Jackson:** Pornography!
Brad: *Playboy* magazine! **Tony:** Best-selling books!
Mike: TV shows! **Renee:** Romance novels!
Andrea: Women's lib! **Jeff:** Rock stars!
Sylvia: Commercials and advertisements!
Kim: Everything!
Glen: Our whole society—exactly. And there's the pressure I

was talking about that was born from the sexual revolution; real freedom says that you have a choice. The sexual pressure from our society says what?

Melissa: That if you're not sexy, you're not anything.

Glen: Right! So we are pressured into acting and looking as sexy as we possibly can, even if we are uncomfortable with that.

Melissa: But mostly women are pressured into acting like that...

Tony: Yeah, but men are supposed to like it—to respond. Men are supposed to be turned on and be real macho—sexy in return.

Glen: Even if they are uncomfortable with that?

Tony: Yeah, man! Otherwise they'd be wimps! *(Realizes as everyone laughs that he's fallen into the trap and says hurriedly)* Well, at least that's what our culture says.

Glen: Right you are.

Todd: Now, what is the loudest voice in our culture teaching men to be sex machines and to treat women as things to be processed? A couple of you mentioned it earlier.

Jackson *(stoutly):* Dirty magazines and pornography!

Todd: Right! Boy, are you sharp tonight! That voice is another result of the so-called freedom we gained through the sexual revolution. Pictures of naked women have always been around, but they were not shown in polite society and ladies and gentlemen did not look at them at all. Isn't it interesting that Jackson used the term "dirty" to describe those magazines? What does that make the men and women who pose for them, and the men and women who look at them?

All: Dirty!

Tony: That description fits perfectly when we consider the message in Ephesians 5:22—28. Jackson, will you read that for us? *(Waits for them all to find it, repeats reference.)*

Jackson *(reads):* "Husbands, love your wives, just as Christ loved the church and gave himself up for her to make her holy, cleansing her by the washing with water through the word, and to present her to himself as a radiant church, without stain or wrinkle or any other blemish, but holy and blameless. In this same way, husbands ought to love their wives as their own bodies. He who loves his wife loves himself."

Todd: The church, of course, is us, so we are the bride of Christ. We are now being prepared to be presented to the bridegroom, who is, of course, Christ. Now, what bride would want to walk down the aisle with huge, ugly, filthy stains on her gown for all to see? When we look at pictures of a sexual nature, whether they are in magazines, in movies, or on TV, they stain our minds with thoughts and images that keep us from being pure—we become blemished.

Glen: Before you continue with that line of thought, I'd like to ask, you guys especially, what message those verses Jackson read have for a married man looking at pornography?

(There is a hustle while those who have Bibles look at the verses again. After a short pause, Jeff raises his hand. With a nod from Glen, he speaks.)

Jeff: This says that a man can show his love for his wife by helping her to be holy, and by loving her as much as he loves himself. Since pornography is degrading to women, a man would not be showing very much respect for his wife if he looked at the stuff. It might even make her feel like she had to degrade herself in order to attract his attention. And I don't know what kind of man thinks so little of himself that he would enjoy looking at degrading pictures of himself.

Glen: That is a very intelligent interpretation, Jeff! And, as a matter of fact, a group called "Women Against Pornography" has found that women report that very thing. Instead of freeing women, the porn explosion has created a new kind of slavery for them because of the abhorant things their husbands now expect them to do. You are *exactly* right! Thanks for letting me add that in, Todd.

Todd: Sure, that's valuable information. Now I want to ask all of you, what besides *pictures* can put lustful thoughts in your mind?

Kim: Some of the same stuff we said before, books, songs, magazines...

Todd: Right. So let's look at a Scripture that tells us what to fill our minds with; Kim, would you read Philippians 4:8 for us, please?

Kim *(stands and reads):* "Finally, brothers, whatever is true, whatever is noble, whatever is right, whatever is pure, whatever is lovely, whatever is admirable—if anything is excellent or praiseworthy—think about such things."

Todd: Thank you, Kim. Now this one, short, simple verse should be the criteria by which we judge everything we put into our minds and spend our time on. Think about how many song lyrics today are noble and pure? How many television shows are true and admirable? How much of your conversation with your friends involves lovely and praiseworthy topics? There is a computer term for this criteria, GIGO. Anyone know what that means and how it applies here?

Mike: It stands for, "garbage in—garbage out," and it means that if we fill our minds with trash, we're going to have trashy thoughts and act in trashy ways.

Todd: Right again. Before we leave the subject of pornography, I want to give you a statistic. The Michigan State Police analyzed the reports of 38,000 sexual assaults that occurred between 1956 and 1979. They found that in at least 41 percent of those crimes, pornography was used or imitated just prior to or during the act. I say "at least" because the percentage could very well have been higher since the question was not asked during all of the investigations. So don't ever fall for the lie that pornography is a private habit that hurts no one. Even without counting these sexual assaults, you and I know that someone was hurt in 100 percent of these cases—who?

All: The man, the guy, the person reading it, whoever looked at it, etc.

Shirley: Right. It's interesting that some of your answers allowed for the fact that women look at pornographic material too. Which brings us to another point. On top of all this cultural influence to have sex, there is something that we have no choice but to look at every day of our lives, and it can elicit a stronger sexual response from us than any other thing we've mentioned tonight. What is it?

(Everyone shouts in unison:)
Boys: Girls! Women!
Girls: Men! Boys! *(Everyone laughs.)*
Shirley: Right again. And wouldn't you know it, there are some Bible verses that speak to this problem. First Timothy 2:9 was written to women. Who wants to read it?
Pete: I will! *(Everyone laughs again.)*
Shirley: Go ahead, Pete!
Pete *(stands and reads):* I also want women to dress modestly, with decency and propriety, not with braided hair or gold or pearls or expensive clothes, but with good deeds, appropriate for women who profess to worship God.
Renee: What's wrong with braids?
Sylvia: Yeah, or jewelry?
Shirley: Timothy was writing to the women of his culture and back then, the only kind of women who braided their hair and dressed to call attention to themselves were you-know-what! *(Laughter.)* The basic message of this verse stands the test of time very well: "dress *modestly,* with *decency* and *propriety."*

It is true that the standards of decency have changed throughout the years. In your great, great grandparents' day, no self-respecting woman would ever let her legs be seen in public and no self-respecting man would take his shirt off in the presence of women. But, wouldn't you say that today's fashion has gone just about as far as it can go with regard to modesty?

I want to tell you a true story about me. I was a teenager back in the 60's when mini skirts became popular for the first time. Now my legs weren't all that great, so I didn't wear the *micro* minis, but my mother nevertheless hassled me daily about the length of my dresses! *(Laughter.)* One night, I was talking with one of the guys in the youth group about how out of it my mother was, and he said to me, "Well, to tell you the truth, I do have trouble sitting next to you in church. All that bare skin makes it pretty hard to concentrate on worshiping God." *(Pause.)* I was shocked and humiliated. This was a guy I had a lot of respect for. It was hard for me then, and is still hard for me to think that I had come between this guy and his worship of God. That experience has *strongly* affected my thinking about what clothes are appropriate—especially in church!

Melissa: Are you saying that it is a girl's fault if a guy gets ideas when he looks at her?

Shirley: What do you think? Read Romans 14:11-13 for us, will you please?

Melissa *(reads)* "'As surely as I live,' says the Lord, 'Every knee will bow before me; every tongue will confess to God.' So then, each of us will give an account of himself to God. Therefore let us stop passing judgment on one another. Instead, make up your mind not to put any stumbling block or obstacle in your brother's way." *(Pause.)* Well, that's pretty plain.

Shirley: OK. Now will somebody please read Matthew 5:27-29? *(Hands go up.)* Go ahead, Amy.

Amy *(finds the verse and reads):* "You have heard it was said, 'Do not commit adultery.' But I tell you that anyone who looks at a woman lustfully has already committed adultery with her in his heart. If your right eye causes you to sin, gouge it out and throw it away. It is better for you to lose one part of your body than for your whole body to be thrown into hell." But that verse is for men—telling them not to be lustful!

Shirley: Don't we have a responsibility to help one another remain pure? What kind of lady is going to purposefully cause men to sin—and why? Because it is good for her ego?

Melissa *(stubbornly):* Well, I can't help it if guys think I'm sexy.

Kim: Oh give it a rest, Melissa! You know that's a cop out! But Shirley, are we supposed to go around in long, black dresses buttoned up to our chin? *(Everyone laughs.)*

Shirley: No, the guideline said, "modestly, with decency and propriety." Accidents may happen; you may buy a new sweater and not realize until the first time you wear it that it is *very* loosely woven, and you need to wear a shirt or a blouse under it. Or, you may be visiting friends and realize when you start to dress for church that you forgot to pack a slip. But if you dress immodestly all the time, you're either ignorant, or you're doing it on purpose. Everyone in this room knows that there are many, many ways that both men and women can dress to call improper attention to their bodies, and the Bible calls that immodest and indecent. And, as we read in Romans 14, we are not ever to be a stumbling block to someone!

Melissa *(sullenly):* Well, what about make-up?

Shirley: Same guidelines apply. I think it's fine to try and look your best, and a little make-up certainly can do wonders! But when you go overboard and begin to look "painted," people wonder what you are trying to prove. We should remember that "painted lady" is another name for a you-know-what! Again, it's simply a matter of drawing too much attention to your face. Let's look at Proverbs 31:30. *(Andrea's hand shoots up.)* Go ahead, Andrea.

Andrea: I know that one! *(Recites:)* "Charm is deceptive, and beauty is fleeting; but a woman who fears the Lord is to be praised."

Shirley: Excellent! Other translations say, "Beauty is vain." What do "fleeting," and "vain" mean?

Renee: "Fleeting" means it doesn't last, and "vain" means you're conceited.

Jackson: No, no. Not in this verse. Well, vain *could* mean "conceited," but I'm pretty sure it means "worthless" and "meaningless."

Shirley: Right. So if physical beauty doesn't last, and is worthless anyway, why strive so hard for it?

Glen: Speaking from a male's point of view, this is all quite confusing.

Kids *(laughing):* Huh? What are you talking about? What? What do you mean? etc.

Glen: I mean, how is a guy supposed to know how to treat a girl when she's dressed and made-up like a hooker, uses vulgar language, tells dirty jokes, and comes on to him like

gangbusters? A lot of times, if he responds to her invitation, she'll act like she's offended!
(The guys all agree, nodding their heads, saying "Yeah," "That's right," etc.
Sylvia: Well you guys aren't too easy to figure out either! You *say* you want a girl who acts like a lady, but the ones you take out are the ones who put out! *We* get the message that nice girls finish last!
(The girls all agree, as the boys did.)
Todd: Interesting situation! Sounds like the old tug of war between spirit and flesh, doesn't it? *(Shirley and Glen nod, some of the kids say, "Huh?")* You know, your mind knows what is right, but worldly pleasures are luring your body onto paths of unrighteousness! *(Everybody laughs.)* At the risk of being executed on the spot, I'd like to suggest that the women's liberation movement is responsible for some of this confusion. *(Girls start to protest.)* Now wait a minute, hear me out. The false promise of the liberation movement was that if women would reject traditional styles of feminine behavior, men would begin to accept them as equals. But in rejecting "feminine" life-styles, woman chose to copy all the worst in men's behavior: swearing, telling dirty jokes, acting vulgar and crude, becoming tough and unforgiving, in short, acting like real macho jerks. And the male macho jerks felt very threatened. That women could take over their jobs was bad enough, now here they were in the boys' beer halls, drinking and telling dirty jokes with the worst of them.
Glen: Some of those macho jerks reacted in anger, and decided to prove their *physical* superiority by knocking women around. *(Everyone gets very serious.)*
Todd: Then you find the situation where too much beer has been flowing and you've got a bunch of confused, insecure, drunk adolescents out to prove something. Along comes an attractive girl who has frequently and openly flirted with them and is very brash about her own sexuality. And the next thing you know, she's become a rape victim. *(Pause.)* Whose fault is it? Certainly the boys. No behavior in the world justifies rape. But can you see how the girl may have planted the idea with her immodest appearance and helped it to grow with her immodest behavior?
Glen: My young friends, there is only one way to get people to treat you like ladies and gentlemen, and I think you know what it is.
Pete: To act like ladies and gentlemen.

Amy *(in shock)*: Who were they?

Mother: They're boys from your school. You probably know them, although I hope they're not the kind you hang around with. I don't have their names, but they're all in jail now, so you'll probably hear soon enough. You'd have heard about it in school today except that it happened so late last night—

Amy: When? What was she doing in the park alone?

Mother: That's what we'd all like to know. Honey, this is *exactly* why your father and I won't let you walk home alone late at night.

Amy: Mom, is she gonna be all right?

Mother: It's too soon to tell. She's in the hospital and has internal injuries. Of course, there's bound to be terrible psychological wounds as well. She's going to need a lot of support from her friends.

(Amy breaks away from her mom and starts pacing around the living room.)

Amy: I won't know what to say to her! This is so awful! Oh, Mom, how many guys were there? Oh man! She *knew* them? *I* know them? I can't believe this—rape! That doesn't happen to people you know—to my friends! Oh Mom! *(She bursts into tears and her mom stands to put her arms around her.)*

Mother: Dear, it's a terrible, terrible fact, but more than three fourths of all rapes are committed by men that the victims know. That's why it's *so* important to really know the boys you go out with, and why your father and I are always so worried about the way you dress—

Amy *(pulls away in anger)*: The way I dress? Are you saying that Janice *asked* for this to happen? Oh Mom! How could you?

Mother: No, no, of course not. There's absolutely no excuse for what those boys did, and they'll probably go to jail for it even though they are juveniles. But Amy, what was she doing out there alone, and why did they call her a tease? Don't you see why it's so important to protect yourself in whatever ways you can? Of course she didn't want such a thing to happen, but many, many people will say that she was inviting trouble—courting danger.

Amy: I can't believe what I'm hearing! Just because Janice doesn't go around in gunny sacks, just because she is *friendly* to people—

Mother: Now Amy, you're upset and you're overreacting. You know there's a difference between modest and immodest dress. And you know there's a difference between being friendly and coming on to guys—

Kim: To *be* ladies and gentlemen.
Glen: And to treat others with the same respect that you desire from them.
(There is a fairly long pause. The kids look thoughtful, the sponsors look concerned.)
Todd: Have we answered any questions tonight?
Amy: Yessss ... but what happened to Janice still isn't right.
Shirley Heavens, no! And it never will be!
Todd: As has been stated many times tonight, rape is never a permissible response. But I hope you will all see that modesty is not an old-fashioned idea that pertains only to women. To be modest means to "have regard for decencies of behavior and dress, to be quiet and humble in appearance, not displaying one's body, not boastful or vain, but unassuming, retiring, virtuous, and reserved." I think that is a description that any person would do well to earn.
Glen: We've covered a lot of ground tonight and we don't want to wear you out. We are glad to have all of you visitors, but sorry about the circumstances that brought you here. Please come back in happier times. Let's close now with a time of prayer together.
(The kids all stand and join hand in one large circle.)
Jackson: Heavenly Father, thank You for being there when hard times hit. Thank You for giving us Your Word, to show us how we're supposed to live.
Amy: Please forgive us, God, for acting and dressing immodestly. I guess we got caught up in a worldly way of thinking and forgot to measure the world's values against Yours. It will be very hard, God, to be different from our friends, and not to wear the latest fashions—if they are immodest. Please give us the courage we need.
Melissa: Heavenly Father, we also need some courage to apologize to our parents. We've been very foolish not to see the concern behind their scolding. Please help me to remember that the next time I'm tempted to get mad at my mother.
Renee: Dear God, please help the whole world to see that all the emphasis on sex is not a good thing. A lot of people are just messin' up their lives trying to be somebody it isn't even worth being. *Please* help them—and us—to see that!
Pete: God, thanks for this church being here so that I could come tonight. It gave me a chance to straighten some things out in my mind.
Tony: God, I guess I'm glad I learned that modesty is for guys, too. I guess I would rather be a gentleman than a—than what

I have been. Thanks for the chance to try again.

Sylvia: Dear Lord, please keep Janice safe and help her to get well. Show us how we can help her too, so that she'll know how many friends she has.

Brad: And Dear God, help us to understand about forgiveness. Those guys are my friends and they're pretty scared right now. I know, and they know, that what they did is terribly wrong, but You can forgive them, can't You?

(Pause.)

Glen: Dear Heavenly Father, we thank You for Your gift of forgiveness. We understand that penalties must be paid and retribution must be made here on earth, but we are so thankful that our sins can be eternally forgiven. Thank You that it is Your will that all will come to You for this salvation. Bless these kids here tonight and help them to stand firm in their decisions. Help us all to understand that growth is a continual process that stops only when we quit trying. Be with us this coming week, Lord, and keep us safe and strong. In Jesus name, amen.

CURTAIN

DISCUSSION QUESTIONS

1. In Romans 12:1 and 2, Paul urges us not to be "conformed to the pattern of this world" but to be "transformed by the renewing of your mind." What does that mean? Could the "renewing of our minds" mean "getting our heads on straight—getting back to God's standards"? The youth group read about God's standards regarding modest clothes and behavior. Do you think that in this world today, we should be able to tell whether or not a person is a Christian by the way he or she dresses? How about the way he or she talks and acts? How do you decide whether or not someone is a "lady" or a "gentleman"?

2. There *are* standards by which others judge us, whether we like that or not. People in the world often have one set of standards for their worldly friends, and a higher set of standards for those who call themselves Christians. Do you think that's fair? Should people be able to expect better behavior from those who say they are followers of Christ? If not, what makes a Christian different from anyone else?

3. Do you think girls ever "invite rape"? Is there any situation or reason to excuse an act of rape? Since rape is generally based on violence, and not lust, does that mean girls should be able to dress any way they want? How does the saying, "Two wrongs don't make a right" apply here?

4. How do you feel about Jackson's inviting his whole class to come to youth group? What would happen at your school if someone did something like that? Do you think Jackson was very brave, to do that?

5. The sponsors pointed out that what some call "liberation" is really enslavement to another master—and that there are high penalties to pay for this type of "freedom." How did people ever come to believe that it would be to their benefit to turn God's value system upside-down? Who do you suppose is responsible for such crafty lies? For help with your answer, look up John 8:43-45.

6. The kids in the play talked about the influence the media had on their lives. Do you think the media influences you that strongly? Why or why not? Where do you get your ideas of fashion and behavior? Are you a "free spirit"—an individual who truly makes his or her own choices? How much do your friends influence your appearance and behavior?

7. "Ladies" and "gentlemen" are kind of old-fashioned terms—they're not titles that we often think about striving for. Yet Lionel Richie sang "Three Times a Lady," and Kenny Rogers sang "She's Always Been a Lady to Me." Does our society still respect ladies? How about gentlemen? Take a poll of the kids in your group. Ask the girls if they'd rather go out with a crude, macho punk rocker or a real gentleman. Ask the guys if they'd rather go out with a flashy, trashy Madonna type or a real lady. If your group prefers ladies and gentlemen, is that what they always act like? If your group prefers punkers and rockers, how do you think you acquired those values?

LIKE A CARELESS MATCH

CAST OF CHARACTERS
Danny Mulligan—high-school student
Mayor of Oaklawn
Ron Graham—principal of Oaklawn High School
Television reporter
Cameraperson
Rick Archer, Rita Archer, Shaun Dickson, Maria Thompson, Lisa—high-schoolmates
Rachel Kerr, Wanda Blessing—adult women
Ruth Reinhart—teacher
Mr. Holt—teacher
Mrs. Holt
Bill, Fred—adult men
Mike Mulligan—Danny's father
Marsha Mulligan—Danny's mother
Betsy Mulligan—Danny's younger sister
Maurice Thompson—Maria's father
Mrs. Thompson—Maria's mother
Brad Thompson—Maria's younger brother
Jeff Thompson—Maria's youngest brother
Alex—youth group leader
Carol—youth group leader
Greg—youth group leader
Youth group kids: Alicia, Robert, Cindy, Walt, plus extras
Extras of all ages to make up audience

SCENES
Act 1 Scene 1: High-school auditorium
Act 1 Scene 2: Mulligan family car
Act 1 Scene 3: Mr. & Mrs. Holt's living room
Act 2 Scene 1: Thompson family dining room
Act 2 Scene 2: School classroom
Act 2 Scene 3: Principal Graham's office
Act 3 Scene 1: Youth-group meeting at church
Act 3 Scene 2: Hall or empty classroom at church
Act 3 Scene 3: High-school auditorium

ACT 1, SCENE 1

The play opens in a high-school auditorium filled with students, parents, and guests, present to see Danny Mulligan be awarded first place in the state competition for Junior Scientist of America. (Danny is an upperclassman of whatever age your group has the most actors and actresses for. Many of his classmates will also have parts.) There is a stage in the back, left corner of your stage, with a speaker's podium front and center. With this arrangement, the speaker on the stage will be facing the real audience as well as the audience on stage, and the audience on stage will not quite have their backs to the real audience. Below the pretend stage, in front of the speaker's podium, are two or more long tables displaying Danny's science project; many bound notebooks containing pages and pages of figures, graphs and charts (use anything—no one in the real audience will be able to see them). Several large charts and graphs done in colored markers show upward curves and ever-larger numbers. Break them up by years, population, amounts of energy saved, etc., whatever looks impressive to you. (You might copy pie charts and bar graphs from the encyclopedia and put new titles on them—again, the real audience will not be able to tell whether or not the charts make sense.) You will also need a big, impressive trophy, a microphone for television reporter and a shoulder-type television camera for cameraman (an oblong box, painted black, with a camera lens in front and heavy black cords coming out of the back).

Mayor: Danny, before I present you with this year's first-place award for the state of _____, I'd like to take just a minute or two to say a few words about your accomplishment. The city of Oaklawn is proud of you today. Your teachers tell me that you're the kind of student they love to have—eager to learn, willing to put out the extra effort it takes to excel—and you've certainly proved that with this winning science project. Your parents tell me you've worked hard for several months, and that you've done it all on your own. The conservation of energy and beating the world hunger problem are topics that concern us all, and you've shown that every individual—every consumer of hot water, every automobile driver, everyone who uses electricity —can cut down on the waste of these energy sources and thereby make more for others. You've given us something to aim for, Danny; the elimination of hunger on this planet. You've shown that if we all do our part to conserve resources, there will be enough for everybody. *(Applause.)*

Our city, indeed our nation, needs more young people with your ambition, your concern for the world and your determination to do the best. You are the type who will grow up to be a solid citizen, a leader in the community, perhaps a scientist who will one day solve the energy and world food problems for all times.

As you all know, Danny wins a $1,000 scholarship to the college of his choice, which, if he invests wisely, should be worth a good deal more by the time he is ready for college. And he wins a trip to New York City for himself and his parents to enter his project in the national competition. And so, Danny, as mayor of Oaklawn, on behalf of the *(state)* school system, and in conjunction with the National Junior Scientists of America, it is with much pride that I present you with the 198_ *(state)* Junior Scientist of America first-place award for a youth project. *(Presents Danny with a big trophy and shakes his hand as the crowd cheers, applauds, stands up, etc. Danny's parents come from beind him to stand with him as newspaper reporters snap photos. As the cheering dies down, Principal Graham steps up to the microphone.)*

Principal Graham: We are indeed all proud of Danny and hope that his industriousness will be an example to the rest of you students. This concludes our awards program for tonight and we thank you all for coming.

(Audience applauds again and people start to leave. Danny comes off the stage towards the edge of the real stage, and reporters gather around him. Other people, adults and classmates, slap him on the back, shake his hand, offer their congratulations. A reporter with a microphone, followed by a TV cameraperson, elbows his/her way up to Danny.)

Reporter: Danny! Excuse me, Danny Mulligan! I'm with station WMOX and I'd like to ask you a few questions for the eleven o'clock news.

(Crowd parts with a few gasps of admiration. Behind him, Danny's mother begins fussing with her hair and dress.)

Danny: Yeah, OK!

Reporter: Can you tell us in just a few words exactly what your project is?

Danny: Well, I researched all the ways that people normally use different forms of energy and then I calculated the cost per individual. Then I started looking at ways people can cut down on their use of energy, and calculated the costs saved individually and collectively. Then I applied those savings to the world hunger problem, and calculated how fast the multiplied savings could end world hunger.

Reporter: Sounds pretty complicated! Can you give us a specific example?

Danny: Yeah, sure. Umm ... let's take water, for example. Water is an energy resource in itself, and then we use oil, gas, or electric energy to heat it up. I thought that we might save some of all four resources if we didn't heat our water so much, or use so much of it.

Reporter: Well Danny, that's very interesting, but people are never going to give up hot water.

Danny: They might when they find out how much they're wasting, and what it's costing them. Did you know that more than four thousand children and adults are hospitalized each year because of burns from scalding tap water in baths and showers?

Reporter: Well, no, I didn't.

Danny: Yep. And too many of them, usually little children, actually die. I determined a cost for medical expenses, loss of work, increased insurance premiums, and costs of funerals, but there is no way I could calculate a cost for heartbreak.

Reporter: Yes, well this is all very interesting, but we're running out of time here ... *(Looks at watch.)*

Danny: Then there's the actual cost of heating the water. 110° to 120° is warm enough for bathing, but most hot water heater manufacturers set the heater thermostats between 140° and 180°.

Reporter: No kidding?

Danny: Nope. When Americans went dishwasher crazy, so did their water bills.

Reporter: Uh, could you explain that please?

Danny: Sure. Automatic dishwasher manufacturers recommend that the hot water temperature be set at 140° in order to scald the dishes. But water that can scald dishes can also burn the skin off a human—so, people have to use more and more cold water to lower the shower or bath water to a temperature they can tolerate. The least expensive thing to do is raise your hot water temperature about thirty minutes before you use the dishwasher, or buy a washer that contains its own heating element.

Reporter: Isn't that expensive?

Danny: Not when you consider the cost of heating *all* the water for your home, year around, to the higher temperature. Then you've got to take into consideration the cost of insulation—to keep that water hot while it travels in pipes all over your house. 130° water pumped thirty feet through a 50° basement loses 22 BTU's per foot in an hour. That adds up to $30—40 a year depending on what kind of heat you use.

Reporter: That's not a lot of money to the average American.

Danny: Ah! But add it up! Say one family saves $40 a year by insulating their water pipes. Say they also cut their consumption of water by two-thirds by installing low-flow faucet aerators on all their faucets, and then they cut their heating bill by 20 percent, simply by lowering the water temperature. For the average American family of four, that's a saving of $146 a year on water and $160 a year on the heating bill. When you start adding in savings from electricity, natural gas, heating oil, and automobile gas conservation, you end up with a figure that should impress anyone! Besides, are you aware of the fact that 65 percent of the world's population goes to bed hungry every night? And that a typical Third-World family has an income of $200 a year?

Reporter: Whoa, Danny! We're off on another subject and out of time! Thanks for explaining your project to the television audience of WMOX. *(Turns to face cameraperson.)* And there you have it, folks. Straight from the mouth of ____-year-old Danny Mulligan, first-place winner of the state-wide Junior Scientist of America competition. *(Reporter continues talking to cameraman as the crowd and Danny move on down stage right. "Danny will now enter his project in the national competition . . .", etc. Reporter fades out. People are clamoring around Danny and his parents, a large group of people including several of Danny's classmates are up at the display tables looking at the project.*

Rick: Can you believe this? *(He gestures toward the project):* Who'd have thought old Mulligan Man had it in him?

Shaun: Not me, that's for sure.

Rita: Oh come off it, Shaun! You're probably just jealous!

Shaun: Jealous!? What would I have to be jealous of? I get straight A's! I've been on the honor roll since we were freshmen!

Rick: Yeah. But you were sorta counting on winning this competition yourself, weren't you?

Shaun *(sarcastically):* I coulda used the scholarship money—sure! And as we all know, Danny Boy doesn't need it! I wouldn't be surprised if his old man greased the way to first place with some big bucks.

Rita: Oh, Shaun, that's ridiculous! I can't believe you'd say a thing like that!

Shaun: Well, I just can't believe Dan won without *some* kind of help! Look at all this stuff. It would take *months* to research and compile these figures—let alone do all the computing!

Rick: Well, I'm sure he used his computer—but there's nothing wrong with that—nothing in the rules about it.

Shaun: Sure! Must be nice to have your own computer, huh?

Rita: Careful, buddy, *I* have my own PC, and so do half the kids in our class. So what?

Shaun: So nothin'! I just never figured Danny Mulligan had it in him to stick to a project like this—and where'd he get the idea? Have you ever known him to come up with an idea that wasn't as dumb as dirt? *(Rick and Rita chuckle.)*

Rick: He *is* pretty slow sometimes—that's for sure!

Rita *(laughing):* Remember in Miss Hanson's class when he gave a report on English sonnets—and used a limerick as an example? *(Everybody laughs.)*

Rick: Yeah! And how about the time he stole the test answers in Mr. Roberts class and copied 'em *word for word* on his answer sheet! *(Rick and Rita laugh uproariously.)*

Rita: And then he couldn't figure out how Mr. Roberts knew he had cheated!

(As Rick and Rita are laughing, a couple of girls on the sidelines move in a little closer in order to hear better. Shaun sticks his hands in his pockets and nods in a knowing manner.)

Shaun: See there? You've just proved my point; once a cheat, always a cheat!

Rick: Oh come on Shaun—that was in the *third* grade.

Shaun *(defensively):* I don't care. It proves he's a cheater.

Rita *(seriously):* Shaun, I'll bet there isn't one person in this school who hasn't cheated at *something, sometime.* You're stretching things pretty far to call Danny a cheater just because of some dumb trick he pulled in the third grade!

(The three of them continue talking as they move offstage. The two girls who were listening move into the places Rick, Rita, and Shaun just left.)

Lisa: Did you hear that? Shaun Dickson thinks Danny cheated to win this award!

Maria: Yeah! I'm not surprised though.

Lisa: You're not? How come?

Maria: I never have liked Danny Mulligan! He thinks he's such hot stuff! He treats me like some kind of loser just because his dad is my dad's boss.

Lisa: He does? I never noticed that. How does he treat you like a loser?
Maria: Oh, you know, he's always *pretending* to be so nice—always says "hello" to me like we were friends or something—when the truth is, I don't even know him.
Lisa: Oh.
Maria: And at the company Christmas party last year I felt like such a *dork!* I mean, my mother made me wear this ridiculous dress, and there was Danny—in a tuxedo!
Lisa: You're kidding! Boy, I'll bet he looked sharp!
Maria: Sharp? He looked like he stepped right off the pages of a fashion magazine! I could have died.
Lisa: But Maria, it's not his fault that you felt like a dork.
Maria: How would you know? Were you there? Did you see how he treated me?
Lisa: No, but—
Maria: But nothing! Quit sticking up for him! He's never done you any favors either *(starts shouting)* and I'm not the least bit surprised to hear that he cheated on this project! *(Several people nearby overhear, gasp, look at the project papers in shock as Maria stomps away. Two adult women begin talking.*
Rachel: Oh my! Wanda, did you hear what she said? Do you think it could be true?
Wanda: True? Well my dear, Maria stated it as a fact, and I guess she's in a position to know.
Rachel: She is? Why's that?
Wanda: Well, don't you know? Her father works in Mulligan's computer company. Why, he probably had to help compile some of this stuff! And he probably felt just terrible doing it. But what can you do when your boss tells you to do something?
Rachel: Well, I can hardly believe that of Mr. Mulligan. He seems like such a fine man—and he *is* an officer in our church!
Wanda: Rachel, you are so naive sometimes! You wouldn't believe what that "fine Mr. Mulligan" has put Maria's poor father through since he bought the company.
Rachel: Oh really? I hadn't heard anything. What has he done?
Wanda: Well! As you know, my Harold works in the personnel department and it just seems that not a week goes by but that Maurice Thompson doesn't get some kind of memo from "President Mulligan" added to his personnel file.
Rachel: Really? What kind of memos?
Wanda: Well! First thing Mulligan does when he takes over is start some kind of advanced technology courses for the

89

employees. Imagine! Maurice has been with that company for twenty years and now all of a sudden he's expected to go back to school!
Rachel: It must have been hard—
Wanda: Hard?! He didn't do well at all! Says he can't get ahold of the new computer language or some such thing. And then Mulligan had the nerve to ask poor Mr. Thompson to relocate. Rachel, can you imagine? Just expected him to pick up his family and move! Mulligan gave him some excuse about his field of expertise being useful in an "older" plant, where they hadn't yet converted to the new computers. Well! You can just bet that Maurice told him "no!"
Rachel: He did?
Wanda: Yes, but Mulligan still wouldn't let him alone. Transferred him to another department and *cut his pay!*
Rachel: Oh no! How awful!
Wanda: Yes, it's just been one thing after another. And now to find out he made poor Maurice work on this spoiled kid's ... stuff!
Rachel *(as the two move off):* I'm shocked! Just absolutely shocked! I guess the church board should hear about this. ...
(Two teachers pick up the conversation.)
Ms. Reinhart: Church board! What about the school board? The rules *clearly* state that all work had to be done by the student, and that the idea was to be an original!
Mr. Holt: Well ... those entries are screened pretty carefully. Just what evidence do we have that the Mulligan boy cheated?
Reinhart: Evidence?! Didn't you just hear Mrs. Blessing say that her husband told her that Old Man Mulligan had forced Maurice Thompson to compile statistics for the kid? Even threatened him with his job!
Holt: Well, it seems like she said something like that. But what makes you think the idea wasn't Danny's?
Reinhart: Have you ever known *Danny Mulligan* to have an idea like *this*?
Holt: No, he never has excelled at anything before—schoolwork or sports, and he's too shy to be popular. I guess I just hoped that this contest would be a new beginning for him.
Reinhart: Quantum leap, wouldn't you say?
Holt: What do you mean?
Reinhart: Well, I mean, really! A kid who has "never excelled at anything" takes first place in a state-wide contest? And goes on to the nationals?

Holt: Anyone could see he was really excited about the topic. Did you hear him during that interview?

Reinhart: Sure he's excited! Who wouldn't be? And there's no doubt that he's done his homework—at least he *knows* what the project is about!

Holt: Now wait a minute, Ruth. We don't know for sure that Danny cheated, but I will admit that it looks pretty suspicious.

Reinhart: Suspicious I guess! You know what they say, "like father, like son."

Holt: What's that supposed to mean?

Reinhart: How do you suppose his father got to where is is today? Probably by climbing all over people—just like he's doing to Maurice Thompson.

Holt: I don't know... I've heard he's a pretty good man to work for.

Reinhart: Humph! You men! Always sticking together! That's just the kind of comment I'd expect from you!

Holt: I'm not defending the man—or the boy! I'm just saying that we ought to check this out.

Reinhart: Yes, I guess we certainly should!

(They drift away and two men take up the conversation.)

Bill: Say Fred, did you hear what those two teachers were talking about?

Fred: No, I wasn't paying any attention. Anything important?

Bill: Well, they seemed to think that maybe the Mulligan boy didn't do this project by himself.

Fred: Oh? Well I doubt that could be true. The judges screen these things pretty carefully. Besides, if Danny's anything like his dad, he'd never even *consider* cheating!

Bill Why's that?

Fred: Mike Mulligan's straight as an arrow. He checks every detail, looks at every possibility—guess that's why he's done so well in computer analysis. His clients know he'll turn every stone to find the right answer. And that's exactly what makes him such a bear to work for! *(Chuckles.)* But I wouldn't have it any other way. I like knowing that my boss is a fair and honest man. Come to think of it, I can see a lot of old man Mulligan in this project here!

Bill: Oh, so you *do* think he helped his kid!

Fred: Naw! I'm just sayin' his kid must be a lot like the old man. Careful, analytical, thorough—shows up in a project like this.

Bill: Those teachers seemed to think that Mulligan had someone at the plant do some of this work.

Fred: You've got to be kidding! No way Mulligan would ask one of us to do something dishonest! Besides, if he did, we'd all know about it.

Bill: What if it was someone who was scared of losing his job?

Fred: Look Bill, how many times do I have to tell you? Mike Mulligan isn't that kind of man. I've never known him to threaten an employee. As a matter of fact, he bends over backwards to help us do our jobs!

Bill: What about Maurice Thompson?

Fred: Thompson! What do you know about him? Never mind—I don't want to know. But he *is* a good example. Thompson's having a hard time of it right now,—I'm not going into the details because I don't like talking about other people's problems—but Mike has done everything in his power to help him keep his job, and Murray has balked every step of the way. Man, a lot of employers would have just let him go, but Mike keeps trying to find a place for him. I tell you, working for Mike Mulligan these past few years has made me wonder if there isn't something to this Christianity of his! You know the man's a straight shooter and you can count on everything he says. Helping his kid break the rules so's he can win a contest just doesn't fit the mold—no way!

Bill: Well, I was just repeating what I heard.

Fred: Yeah? Well it sounds like a lot of hot air to me. People shouldn't go around sayin' stuff like that. The kid could take the rap for it!

Bill: Yeah, Fred, guess you're right about that.

END OF SCENE 1

ACT 1 SCENE 2

The Mulligan family car is en route home. Two chairs in front, three in back (or a bench) will give the idea of a car. Mr. Mulligan can hold a steering wheel in his hands, or you can get elaborate and put car seat covers on your chairs, create a console between Mr. and Mrs., and affix the steering wheel to a cardboard dash. The family should bounce or sway a little, but not so much as to distract attention from the dialogue. The trophy is riding prominently between Danny and Betsy.

Mr. Mulligan: Well, Son, I guess you know, but I don't mind telling you again, that we're pretty proud of you.

Mrs. Mulligan: We sure are! Oh Danny, I just thought I'd burst with pride at the way you handled that television interview— you were so *confident* and self-assured!

Betsy: Yeah, you were cool, Dan! I could hardly believe it was you!

Dan *(laughing)*: Thanks! Coming from you, that's a pretty high compliment! I guess I was just so excited about winning that I hardly stopped to think about being on television. Anyway, it was a really good chance to tell more people about the need to conserve energy and spread the wealth.

Betsy: Oh, spare us, please! If I hear one more word about world hunger—

Mrs.: It *has* been a long haul, Dan, but I must say, you certainly stuck with it!

Mr.: Yes, he certainly did that! Maybe now *I'll* get some time on the home computer again!

Mrs.: And I won't have to clean charts and diagrams off the kitchen table every time I want to use it.

Danny *(still laughing)*: You've all been great! Hey! Those guys at the Academy Awards are right—I couldn't have done it without you! If you hadn't been so supportive, and—

Betsy: And if *I* hadn't loaned you all my art markers—

Dan: Yes, and showed me how to do an attractive diagram—listen, I just want to thank you all. You've been just great and, well, I'm just really glad that I have a family like you.

(Mrs. Mulligan wipes her eyes with a hankie, Mr. Mulligan clears his throat, and then Betsy says,)

Betsy: Oh boy! Let's don't get carried away here! Talk about mush!

(Everybody laughs. Mr. Mulligan pulls the car up to the curb and turns off the ignition. Everyone falls silent.)

Mr.: All joking aside Dan, we know how much work the project was, and how hard you've worked on it. And even if you hadn't won, you've discovered a field that you're really interested in, and I'd say you've got a good start on a thesis for a environmental engineering degree.

Mrs.: Or maybe you could submit an article to *Reader's Digest,* or some religious magazine?

Betsy: Or maybe we could just go in and get some ice cream?

(Everybody laughs again and starts to open imaginary car doors.)

Mrs.: Wait! Wait! Before this rare moment of family unity is over, shouldn't we thank the One who made all this possible?

Dan: Good idea, Mom. I've been feeling like I'd like to pray all night—sorta like I want to share all this good stuff with God.

Mr.: Well then, let's do it! *(Everybody settles back into the car.)*

Betsy: I'll start! *(Family chuckles, says "OK" etc. All bow their heads.)* Dear God, thank You for this wonderful night, and for the award that Danny won, and for the way he was able to act on television. Thank You for giving him the energy to finish his project and thank You that we're the kind of family who can stick together during something like this.

Dan: Father God, I *do* want to share all my joy with You because I know that You're partly responsible for my winning. If we hadn't studied about world hunger at youth group, and if I hadn't known how important it is to You that we share what we have, I think I might have given up on this project a couple of times. I just pray now that more and more people will see the importance of conserving and sharing what they have.

Mrs.: Heavenly Father, thank You so much for my family and for the special young man that Danny is growing up to be. We're all so proud of him tonight and pray that You are too— that You are pleased with what he's done. Use this project, Lord, to make more people aware of *all* of Your world.

Mr.: Thank You for the many blessings of today, Lord. Help us always to live our lives so that we can be proud of one another, and You can be proud of us. Thank You for giving me a son who cares enough about world problems to try and do something about them. We all pray in Jesus' blessed name. Amen.

(They get out of the car and start for the house walking away from the audience. Everybody is in a great mood. Lights begin to dim. Danny throws his arms up toward the sky and yells.)

Dan: Wow! Have you ever seen such a *beautiful* night? I can't remember ever being happier in my life!

(Betsy punches him and starts running. He runs after her, laughing. Mr. and Mrs. Mulligan wrap their arms around each other's waists and continue toward the house as the lights go down.)

END OF SCENE 2

ACT 1 SCENE 3

(Lights come up on Mr. Holt's living room. He is talking on the phone.)

Mr. Holt: Yes sir. Yes, it is unbelievable. But I thought you'd want to know as soon as possible so we can get the investigation started. *(Pauses.)* Oh, I don't know. Mrs. Maurice Thompson seems to know something about it ... and some of Danny's closest friends. You might ask Rick and Rita Archer, and Shaun Dickson, and maybe the Thompson girl. But sir, I really hope you'll give Danny the benefit of the doubt. He's been a fine student for as long as I've known him. He's not as naturally gifted as some of the others, but he always works hard and I've never known him to be dishonest. *(Pauses.)* Yes sir, I know. Those quiet ones can fool ya. *(Pauses.)* Well, OK. I'll wait for your instructions. *(Pauses.)* You're welcome. I guess I'll see you Monday. Good night. *(Hangs up, puts his head in his hands. His wife comes into the room.)*

Mrs. Holt: Did you call Principal Graham?

Mr. Holt: Yeah. Just hung up. That's one of the hardest calls I've ever had to make!

Mrs. Holt: I know, Dear. I'm really disappointed in Danny, too. He seems like such a *nice* boy.

Mr. Holt: Yeah, I know. But the part I can't get over is Mr. Mulligan's treatment of Maurice Thompson. *(Sighs.)* With an example like that, it's no wonder that Danny's turning out the way he is. And, I guess when you've got money, you get pretty used to taking the easy way out.

Mrs. Holt: Well, there'll be no easy way out of this mess, that's for sure! As sorry as I am about Danny, I hope the school board will come down hard—really make an example out of him! It's time these kids learn you can't cheat your way through life.

Mr. Holt: Yeah. I guess you're right.

END OF ACT 1

ACT 2 SCENE 1

Evening of the next day. Dinner table of the Thompson household. Mrs. Thompson is setting dishes of food on the table. Marie, her two younger brothers, and Mr. Thompson are already seated.

Marie: You'll never guess what happened at school today! Boy! It was great!

Brad *(excitedly):* What?

Marie: Well, it doesn't concern *you*. I was talking to Mom and Dad.

Maurice: Don't talk to your brother like that, Marie. Now what could possibly happen at your school that I would find exciting?

Marie *(importantly):* Danny Mulligan was accused of cheating on his science project—that's what! And they say his *father* helped him!

(Mr. and Mrs. Thompson look at each other as if a bomb hit the house. Mrs. Thompson sits down on the edge of her chair.)

Mrs. T: Why, who would say a thing like that, Dear? Who accused him? What's going to happen to him?

Marie *(confused):* Well, I dunno. *Everybody* was talking about it. Of course, *I* heard it last night at the award ceremony. I guess word finally got back to Mr. Graham today. Danny will probably get called into his office tomorrow.

Mr. T *(tiredly, self-pityingly):* Well, I'm not surprised. Old man Mulligan seems to think he can have everything else his own way—why not a contest for his son?

Marie *(triumphantly):* That's *exactly* what I said!

Mrs. T: You said?! To whom? And where?

Marie: You know, to some of the kids when we were talking about it.

Mr. T: Just what, exactly, did you say, Marie?

Marie: I don't remember! Just that Danny is stuck on himself—like his Dad—and that they think they can buy anything or anyone!

(Mr. and Mrs. look carefully at each other again. Mrs. T dishes up some food for her closest son and herself, then hands the bowl to Marie.)

Mrs. T: Marie, dear, I'm sure you know better than to repeat in public anything that Daddy and I discuss privately.

Brad: You mean about Daddy being in trouble at work?

(Parents look at him in shock.)

Mr. T: Bradley, I am *not* in trouble at work! There have been a few minor problems between me and Mr. Mulligan, but everything is working out! *(To Marie.)* And yes, that is exactly the type of discussion we mean.

Marie: Well, don't get on *my* case. I hear Mom talking about it on the phone almost every day.

Mrs. T: Marie!

Marie: Well you do! You and Mrs. Blessing talk about it all the time.

Mrs. T: That is *not* the same as blabbing in public! Mrs. Blessing's husband works in personnel at your daddy's plant, and she can tell us . . . things.

Marie: Oh, I get it—sorta like "all in the family," huh?

Mr. T: Marie, I don't care a bit for your attitude. Now I want to know exactly what you said to those kids, and I want to know right now!

Marie *(whining):* I told you, Daddy! I just said he was stuck up and that I wouldn't be surprised if his dad *did* help him with the project.

Mr. T: You didn't mention me?

Marie: No, why should I?

Mr. T: You shouldn't! That's just my point! *(Looks around the* table greatly relieved.) Now, let this be a lesson to all of you *(shakes his finger); never* repeat private family business to anyone outside the family! Get it? *(Everyone nods.)* Well then, let's eat.

Jeff: Aren't we going to pray, Daddy?
Mr. T *(embarrassed):* Uh, I don't feel much ... why *sure* we are Jeffie! As a matter of fact, we'll let *you* pray tonight.
(Jeff beams as everyone bows for prayer.)

END OF SCENE 1

ACT 2 SCENE 2

School classroom between classes. Kids are milling around rows of desks talking, laughing, goofing off. As Dan Mulligan enters the room and kids notice him, they fall silent, group by group, until Danny is left winding his way to his seat in total, absolute silence. Danny is really embarrassed. He sits down in front of Shaun, plops his books down and turns in the chair to face the audience. Shaun is on his left. Gradually, as Shaun and Dan talk, the groups resume talking (miming).

Dan: *Hey, Shaun!*
Shaun: Hey, Dan!
Dan: Boy, this is weird! Yesterday everyone was congratulating me and treating me like some kind of hero, and today they all act like I'm a goon from the Twilight Zone.
Shaun: Whaddaya mean?
Dan: Well, I guess it was too much to expect the hero treatment to last, but it seems to me like nobody even wants to mention the Science Fair prize today. The only person to speak to me was some eighth grader who I don't even know. He said that he'd seen me on the news. Everyone else acts like I fell off the face of the earth.
Shaun: Maybe you just fell off the pedestal.
Dan: What's that supposed to mean?
Shaun: Aw, nothin'. They're probably just jealous. I wouldn't worry about it if I were you.
Dan: Yeah, you're probably right. And after all, I don't want to get the big head about this. Still, even my closest friends—
Shaun *(defensively):* Well whaddaya want? That we should fall down at your feet or something? *(Kids nearby snicker.)*
Dan *(embarrassed):* Aw Shaun, gimme a break. *(He turns to face front.)*
Shaun *(leans forward):* Well *maybe* everybody is ignoring you today because they've decided you didn't *earn* the award.

Dan *(turns halfway around):* What do you mean? I won it didn't I? My project was selected by the judges, wasn't it?

Shaun: Yeah, well, that's just it. Nobody can figure you for a winner. *(Dan starts to get angry.)* Now just a minute—don't get excited! It's just that you've sorta always been a guy in the background and some of us—I mean some of them—were wondering how you happened to win.

Dan: What's *that* supposed to mean? Do *they* think my dad *bought* the judges or something?

Shaun *(leans back with a self-righteous look on his face):* You said it Danny Boy, not me.

Dan *(turns angrily to face Shaun head-on):* Well that's just plain ridiculous! Even if the judges *could* be bought, my dad would never do a thing like that! He would never even consider it! *(Short pause.)* Hey you know, *(shakes a finger at Shaun)* that is as much an insult to my dad as it is to me!

Shaun: Hey! Don't take it out on me! I'm not the one saying these things! I just thought that, as a friend, I ought to tell you what people are saying.

Dan: Yeah. Right. *(Pauses.)* Look, I'm sorry Shaun, but that just makes me pretty mad. *(Pauses.)* What *else* are they saying?

Shaun: Oh, you know, the usual stuff—like maybe you had help with the project, or that it wasn't an original idea.

Dan *(gives a snort):* Well, *you* of all people know the answer to that! How many of your games did I miss because I had to work on my project? How many times did I stay home while the rest of you guys went to the mall? *You* saw the papers and books and computer printouts all over my room. You saw how much work it was!

Shaun: Well sure, Dan, and that's what I've been telling people too—whenever they ask. Don't worry, *I'm* your friend. I'll stick by you.

Dan: Thanks. *(Pauses.)* Listen, I guess it was hard for you to tell me that stuff, and, well, I guess I do appreciate knowing what's going on. But it does make me sick! What kind of people would start such awful lies?

Shaun *(looks miserable by now):* Aw, you know how *some* people are. *(Both boys are quiet for a moment, then Shaun brightens up)* But hey, Dan, I never did congratulate you either! You're right, I *do* know how much time you spent on this project, and how important it was—is—to you, and I'm really glad you won!

Dan *(lightens up a little):* Thanks, Shaun. That means a lot to me right now. I just hope these rumors die down fast—before I

get into big trouble.
Shaun *(worried):* I do too, Danny, I do too!
(Ms. Reinhart enters the room and everyone quiets down.)
Ms. Reinhart: Danny Mulligan, I have a message here *(waves a slip of paper)* that says Principal Graham would like to see you in his office right away. *(Kids around the room mock, "Aha! You're in trouble now!" etc. Ms. Reinhart speaks up hastily.)* I imagine it's about your award—um, maybe he wants to personally congratulate you or something.
Dan *(gathering up his stuff):* Yes ma'am. I imagine it is. *(Mumbles to Shaun.)* And right now, I don't know whether to be excited or scared.
(As he leaves the room, Ms. Reinhart looks a little sad, Shaun looks worried and scared, and the rest of the kids look self-righteous, unconcerned, or are laughing at Dan.)
Ms. Reinhart *(snaps to a professional manner):* All right now, class, let's get down to business.
(Class groans, shuffles books, opens notebooks as lights go down on classroom and up on principal's office.)

END OF SCENE 2

ACT 2 SCENE 3
(Principal Graham, Mr. Holt, and Danny's parents are seated in the room as Danny enters.)
Dan: Mom! Dad! What are you doing here?
Mr. Mulligan: I don't know, Son. Mr. Graham called me at work and asked me to meet him here at 11:30, so here I am.
(Danny looks wonderingly at his mother.)
Mrs. Mulligan *(shrugs):* Me, too. I was just leaving to get groceries when he called.
Principal Graham *(clears his throat):* Well now! I won't keep you in suspense any longer. Danny, have a seat. *(Gestures toward a chair in front of his desk. As Danny sits, Mr. Graham gets up and starts pacing back and forth behind his desk.)* Danny, this is very difficult for me to say. As you know, I was very proud of you at the awards ceremony Friday night. Your winning science project brought national recognition to this town, and to our school. And, your scholarship money was to be matched by the state with a gift to the science department. Now, it seems that we might be in danger of losing all that, and that you have brought a terrible shame upon yourself, your family, and this school.
(At the words "danger of losing" Danny and his parents start

whispering "What?!" and become very agitated.)
Dan (half stunned): Mr. Graham, I don't, I don't know what—what you're talking about—
Mr. Mulligan (half out of his chair): See here, Graham, what's this all about? I think you'd better clarify things a little. (Mrs. Mulligan reaches over to pat his arm, he settles back into his chair as Mr. Graham continues.)
Principal: *I was just about to*, Mr. Mulligan. It seems your son here has been accused of cheating on his project, (all three Mulligans gasp, react in different shocked ways) and *you* have been accused of helping him by using manpower and computer time at your company!
(The Mulligans are speechless. They look from each other to the principal, and back to Danny. Finally, when all attention is focused on him, Danny speaks.)
Dan: Mr. Graham, I didn't cheat. My parents know how hard I worked on my project. And Dad helped me program some stuff, but that was at home on our own computer, and he just helped me figure out the program—not with actual research and computing . . . that's OK, isn't it?
Mr. Mulligan (speaking to Principal): See here, Ron, this is perfectly ridiculous. Who has accused us of such things?
Principal: Well, pretty nearly the whole school is talking about it. I received several calls from irate parents over the weekend, and quite a few this morning. One of the most disturbing calls was from a (consults a page of notes on his desk) Mrs. Rachel Kerr. Seems she's a friend of Wanda Blessing, whose husband works in your personnel department, (Mr. Mulligan nods) and it seems that this Harold Blessing saw one of your men working on Danny's project.
Mr. Mulligan (jumping out of chair): What?! Why, that's absurd. That's a lie! That's libelous! And it's *easily* proven false. You just call Harold Blessing—better yet, *I'll* bring him down here! I can't believe he'd say such a thing. In fact, I don't. Who is he supposed to have seen working on Danny's project?
Principal: Well, uh, (consults notes again) that would be a Mr. Thompson.
Mr. Mulligan: Maurice?! (Looks quickly at his wife, takes a deep breath and sits back down.) Well now, this is beginning to make sense. Ah, Ron, I don't like to discuss personnel with uninvolved parties, but I've been having a little bit of trouble with Maurice Thompson lately. I think if you and I just speak to him privately, we can get to the bottom of this.
Principal: Believe me, I *intend* to speak to every person

involved here. But that still doesn't answer the accusation that this project was not an original idea of Danny's.
(Every eye in the room turns to Danny. He squirms in his chair. Mr. Holt speaks for the first time.)
Mr. Holt *(kindly):* Well, Danny, where *did* you get the idea?
Dan: I . . . I don't know. I mean it just sort of grew. I read some stuff in one of Mom's magazines about home insulation . . . and about children who get scalded with hot water at home . . .
Holt: You *read* about this in a magazine? *(Looks meaningfully at the principal.)*
Principal *(clears his throat again):* Uh, Danny, I think you'd better bring this article in to me.
Dan *(shouts):* No! I mean, it wasn't even the same article! I read one thing in one magazine, and one in another, and I remembered reading in an old *Reader's Digest* about how much money could be saved with conservation, and I tried to find that article at the library, but I couldn't and I just started imagining different ways to conserve energy and wondering how much money could be saved if the whole nation would do it, and, and, *(breaks down)* Mr. Graham, I didn't copy anybody's idea. I didn't cheat!
(Everyone is silent for a moment, studying Danny. Mrs. Mulligan gets up, walks over and lays her hand on Danny's shoulder.)
Mrs. Mulligan: Mr. Graham, Mr. Holt, I believe my son. *(She looks at her husband and he nods.)* We both do. What Danny has just described to you is the birth of his idea, and the research that followed. It's permissible, isn't it, that his idea for a project on conservation came from several things he read?
Principal: Yes, ah, yes. I think that's permissible. After all *(weak chuckle)* there's really nothing new under the sun! *(Short pause.)* But you have to understand that I had Danny's previous record to consider. *(More surprised looks on the Mulligan's faces.)*
Mr. Mulligan *(joins his wife):* And what record would that be, Ron?
Principal *(consults notes again):* It seems there was a little matter of stolen test answers in a Mr. Roberts' class—I don't believe that was at this school since I don't have a Roberts on staff—
Dan: Mr. Graham! Mr. Roberts was my *third grade* teacher! And yes, I did steal those test answers! That was just about the dumbest thing I've ever done, and the last time in my life that

101

I ever cheated! *(He slumps down in his chair, his mother gives him a pat and goes to sit in her chair. Mr. Mulligan steps around to Graham's desk.)*

Mr. Mulligan: Ron, we punished Danny pretty severely for that, and he took a grade lower on his report card because of it. But frankly, I'm a little amazed that something a boy did as a nine-year-old would throw such a big shadow on his character. *(Mr. Graham and Mr. Holt look embarrassed.)* Dan learned a big lesson from that experience, and I believe him when he says he's never cheated again. Besides that, I *saw* the amount of work my boy did on that project! But, *(Dan and Mrs. Mulligan look up in surprise)* just for the record. ... *(he walks to Dan's chair)* Son, you know how disappointed your mother and I will be if there is any truth to these accusations. *(Dan nods.)* But you also know that we'd be even *more* disappointed in you if you are lying now to cover something up. *(Danny looks sick—disbelieving—stunned.)* As hard as it would be—harder than anything you've ever had to do in your life—would you tell me now, tell all of us, if you did any cheating?

(Dan looks up at his dad, his mother, Mr. Holt, and the principal. Finally he gets up from the chair and faces his dad.)

Dan *(hands clenched behind his back):* Dad, I don't know what's going to happen to the award, or the scholarship money, or anything. I do know that the winning has already been ruined for me. Everyone in the school—everyone in the whole town—seems to believe I'm a cheater. But Dad, Mom, I can stand here and look you in the eye with God as my witness, and tell you *I did not cheat!* I'm willing for Mr. Graham to go through all my papers and research notes—you know that the prize committee already has. He can look at anything he wants, ask questions of everyone he wants, *do* anything he wants, because I have nothing to hide. I did not cheat!

(Mr. Mulligan grins and sticks out his hand for a shake. As they shake, Mr. Mulligan pulls Danny in for a hug and then turns to Mr. Graham and Mr. Holt, with his arm still around Danny's shoulders.)

Mr. Mulligan: Gentlemen, that's good enough for me! You go ahead and complete whatever investigation you feel you have to, but my wife and I will back Danny all the way. And now, if you don't mind, I think we all ought to get back to what we had planned for the day.

(Graham nods, Mr. Mulligan shakes hands and says "good-bye" to both men. Mrs. Mulligan leaves with her arm around Danny.

Mr. Mulligan follows. They walk offstage as Graham speaks.)
Principal: Holt, I've got a bad feeling about this. I just *can't* believe that boy is lying. I've known Mike Mulligan for twenty-five years and he's a good, honest, and decent man. Can't believe he'd raise a boy to be a cheater, let alone help him cheat. And, I can't believe he'd be fool enough to cover for him either. *(Pauses.)* Will you help me get to the bottom of this? We've got to talk to every single person on this list and see where these accusations started and if there's any truth to 'em. Frankly, I think it's a waste of time.
Mr. Holt: Yes sir, Mr. Graham, I'm inclined to agree with you. It's a distasteful mess, but I'm willing to help you clean it up.
(Lights go down on the office and up on Danny and his parents in the school hall.)
Dan: Mom, Dad, thanks for sticking up for me. I don't think I could have stood it if *you* didn't believe me either!
Mrs. Mulligan: It's an awful thing to have happened, Danny. I'm just so sorry!
Dan: To tell you the truth, Mom—ha! *That* expression never meant so much! *(All chuckle.)* Well, the truth is, I feel kinda sick about this and I'd like to go home. *(Mrs. Mulligan nods sympathetically.)* I mean, the whole school hates me, and I'd just as soon not have to face anymore of them today.
Mrs. Mulligan: Why, I think it'll be OK for Danny to take the afternoon off, don't you, Dear?
Mr. Mulligan: No . . . no, I don't. *(Dan and Mom look surprised.)* If you leave, Dan, your schoolmates are going to think you're running, and they'll think that if you're running, you have something to hide. No, I think it's best that you tough it out right here. If you think it will help, put a sign around your neck that says "I did not cheat." *(All three laugh weakly.)* Well, all joking aside, I know I'm asking you to do a hard thing, and I know you can use some help—
Mrs. Mulligan: So let's ask for some!
(Danny nods, the three join hands and bow their heads.)
Mr. Mulligan: Father, we know You're with us through this trial. Just now we ask that You'd give Danny the courage to face his classmates, some of whom must have started these rumors.
Mrs. Mulligan: And Father, we pray that You will also give Danny and us the strength and love to forgive those who are responsible for this. Please protect him now as he goes back to face the teachers and students.
Dan: Dear God, this is the hardest thing I've ever gone through.

Please help me get through it. And thank You, because I know You already have and will continue to help me.
Mr. Mulligan: We pray these things, knowing that You love us. In Jesus' name, amen.
(Mrs. Mulligan hugs Danny, puts a hankie to her eyes and leaves. Mr. Mulligan hugs him, and follows her out. Danny stands with his hands in his pockets, back to the audience, watching them leave as the curtain comes down.)
END OF ACT 2

ACT 3 SCENE 1
Sunday night youth group. Rick, Rita, Shaun, Danny, Alicia, Robert, Cindy, Walt, and Betsy are all present, along with some other kids. Danny is sitting off to the side by himself. Betsy is with some of her friends but she keeps looking worriedly at Danny. No one else looks at him and everyone is pretty quiet. The youth sponsors walk in—two men (Alex and Greg) and a woman (Carol).

Alex *(with enthusiasm):* Well! You are a strangely quiet bunch tonight. Somebody die? *(There are a few half-hearted chuckles.)* No?
Greg: No, I think it's more like they all just lost their best friend. *(Dan and Shaun look up in shock. Everybody else looks puzzled and curious. A few murmurs of "what's he talking about? Beats me—I dunno," etc., are heard.)*
Carol: Now look. We could all pretend that we don't know what's going on here, but we do—so what do you say we talk it over? Danny, would you mind?
Dan: I'd really rather that we didn't.
Walt: Why? You got something to hide?
Alex: Now just a minute, Walt. That is not exactly the kind of talk we had in mind. I think—
Dan: Wait Alex, I'd like to answer Walt's question. *(He gets up from his place alone and walks to the front of the room, shoves his hands into his pockets.)* Maybe we *should* talk about this mess. I know I'd sure like to tell the whole city a few things! Walt, maybe your question is fair because you haven't been around here very long and you don't know me very well. You don't have too many reasons to doubt what you've heard, so I just want to tell you that no, I have nothing to hide. I want to tell *all* of you, *and* your parents, *and* the school board, *and* the contest committee, no! I did not cheat. But you know what? I don't think I'd feel any worse tonight if I did! Do you

have any idea how awful it is to have the whole town think you're a liar and a cheat? And not only you, but your dad, too? *Somebody* had to start this rumor. I'm angry about that, but you know what? I just mostly feel sorry for that person or persons—whoever they are. As bad as it is for me, at least I *know* that I'm innocent. How do you think that person must feel?

Betsy: Uh, Danny, excuse me, but that person—or people—might not even realize what they've started. You know, it's what Mom calls "idle gossip." Someone says something without thinking and doesn't even stick around to see what damage it does.

(While she is talking, Danny goes back to his place and sits down.)

Alicia: I suppose that's possible, but I'll bet the person who started these rumors was jealous.

Cindy: Yeah! Envy can make you do and say some pretty awful things—I know.

Rick: Sometimes people don't even mean to get something started—sometimes they're just talking to fill the void.

Walt: Hey! Get real, will ya? Ten minutes ago you all thought Danny was guilty. Why the sudden change of heart?

Alicia: Well, I didn't *really* believe Danny had cheated, but you know, it's awfully hard to buck the crowd. I mean, what if I was the only one who believed that Danny was innocent and I turned out to be wrong?

Walt: Oh wow! That's really brave, Alicia!

Betsy: Are you calling *her* a coward? I'll tell you who's really a coward! I am! I'm Danny's sister and I never doubted him for one minute. I *saw* too much of the mess in our house for too long to think that Danny was getting any outside help with this project—but did you see *me* sticking up for him? Was I over there sitting with him when no one else would? *(Turns to her brother.)* Danny, I'm really sorry, please forgive me. I shouldn't have left you to handle this by yourself. *(She goes over to sit with him. Shaun and Rick and Rita are sitting with their heads down so no one can see their faces. All the kids are really quiet.)*

Carol: I know this is really hard, but look—you've brought up several reasons why people gossip. *(Ticks them off on her fingers.)* Meaningless talk, envy, jealousy, lack of a *real* relationship with the victim, peer pressure. What are some other reasons why people go along with gossip?

Robert: I think people gossip just because it's exciting. *(Othe* say "Huh?" "What are you talking about, man?") Well look at all the excitement this has caused! I mean if Danny had just won the award and that was it, we probably wouldn't even be talking about it tonight, but as it is, the whole town is talking! *(Several kids chuckle.)*

Greg: That's a good point Robert. But what makes people so willing to get such "excitement" at another person's expense?

Dan *(jumps up in anger):* I'll tell you what—I don't *care* about the people who don't know me. What I want to know is, how come people who *do* know me have turned their backs on me? *(Pause. Moves around the room.)* The preacher came to our house this afternoon. He just heard about this mess after church this morning, and he came over right after lunch. And you know what he did? He walked in the door, hugged me, and said, "Danny, anybody can make a mistake, and I don't know whether you did or not, but I want you to know that I think you're a fine young man and I love you. Now tell me, did you cheat?" When I told him "no," he just grinned from ear to ear and said, "I was sure I'd hear that answer!" Then he sat down with us and just talked about this mess, and before he left he prayed with us, and what I want to know is, how come he's the only one? There are some people here who are supposed to be my best friends—oh, man! I gotta get outta here! *(Danny leaves the room in a rush—it looks like he may be crying. After a stunned moment, Betsy starts to go after him. Shaun stops her at the door.)*

Shaun: Wait a minute, Betsy. I think it's time that I—*(stops, runs his hand through his hair)* Whew! I think it's time for me to start acting like a friend. I've got some explaining to do, and I think I'd better start with Dan. *(He leaves the room. Betsy turns back and several kids start questioning her.)*

Cindy: What's going on?

Robert: What's he talking about?

Alicia: Sounds to me like Shaun's involved in this mess!

Rita *(stands up and walks out into the middle of the group, arms outstretched, palms up—like a traffic cop):* Now wait just a minute! Hold it! Stop right there! *(She drops her arms and looks around at the group.)* Haven't we learned *anything* from this mess? Let's not start guessing and talking about stuff that we don't know anything about! What Shaun has to say to Danny is their business.

Right! And even if they *do* tell us what they're talking we don't necessarily need to discuss it or pass it along,

right? *(The group nods in agreement.)*
Alex: Well, this is great! You guys are pretty smart. *(Chorus of groans.)* No! I'm not kidding! There are a lot of adults in this world who haven't yet learned when to keep their mouths shut—a lot of people who think everything they hear, whether true or not, is worth repeating to someone else. If you all have figured out, this early in your lives, that speculation and "curiosity" are cousins to gossip, I'd say you're doing pretty well!
Greg: I'll second that, and make a motion that we close the discussion! Nominations are now open for some songs you'd like to sing.
(A clamor begins as kids are shouting out the names of songs, and the lights go down on the youth group.)

END OF SCENE 1

ACT 3 SCENE 2

Semi-dark empty hallway or classroom in the church building (whatever is easiest for you to stage). Should be a couple of chairs or a bunch. Lights come up only halfway, to reveal Danny with his back to the audience, leaning up against the wall. Hands are shoved into pockets. He stands there alone for a while, then Shaun enters, looking miserable. He sees Danny, stops and hangs his own head, then looks up toward Danny.

Shaun: Uh, Dan? Danny, I—

Danny *(holds out his hand in a "stop" position):* Shaun, I'd really just like to be left alone for a while, ya know?

Shaun: Sure, sure, I understand. *(Starts to turn away, stops, turns back again.)* But Danny, I, uh, I really need to talk to you.

Dan: You need to talk to me *right now?*

Shaun: Yeah. It's important.

Dan: OK. *(Shrugs his shoulders.)* What's so important?

Shaun: *(comes a little closer):* Dan, uh, I don't know how to say this ... uh, about that rumor that you cheated on your project?

Dan: Yeah?

Shaun: Well, I, uh, oh man, I feel really bad about it!

Dan: You do? Well, that's nice to hear, I suppose.

Shaun: No, man, wait. I think I'm—man! You have every right to be really mad at me!

Dan: Shaun, what *are* you talking about? Why don't you spit it out?

Shaun: I'm trying to! What I'm trying to tell you is that I think, maybe, I think, I might be responsible for the rumor.

Dan: What?! *(Pauses.)* You? *(Pauses.)* Why??

Shaun: Oh Dan, I didn't mean to! I was just mouthing off after the ceremony. I guess I *was* jealous—I don't know. I didn't intend to hurt you. I never had any idea things would go this far! I was just blowin' off steam to Rick and Rita—but they didn't agree with me then, and they didn't repeat what I said. I've already asked them. I guess some other blabbermouth must've overheard. *(Shaun runs dry and holds out his arms, palms up, in a shrug of "I don't know.")*

Dan *(looks at Shaun in silence for a moment):* Just what, exactly, did you say?

Shaun: Oh man! I don't even know. I'm too ashamed to tell you what I do remember! I said something about you never winning anything before and I wondered how you won this one—

108

I, I said you were too dumb to come up with an idea like that—but Danny, *(rushing, pleading)* I didn't mean it! I don't know *why* I said those things! It was just plain stupid, and, and, I am so sorry, man!

Dan *(after some silence):* Look Shaun, I don't know what you expect me to say—"No problem? No harm done?"

Shaun: No, no. I know things are in a terrible mess, and I guess it's all my fault. I mean, it looks like some other people were running off at the mouth too, but I guess I must have been the first. *(Pauses.)* Look, is there anything I can do to make this up to you?

Dan *(after a pause):* Yes, you can go to Mr. Graham and tell him what you just told me.

Shaun *(shoulders slump):* Oh, man! *(Collects himself again.)* OK—I will! First thing in the morning, I promise.

Dan: OK. That'll help.

Shaun: Uh, Dan? Do you think things will ever be OK between us again? I mean, will you ever be able to—uh, be my friend?

Dan: Do you mean, will I be able to forgive you?

Shaun: Yeah. Yeah, I guess that's what I mean.

Dan: Well, I want to. I guess I can. It'll probably take a while till I feel good about you, but I know you didn't mean for anything awful to happen.

Shaun: No! I sure didn't!

Dan: Well, I guess we've all said things we later wish we hadn't. Luckily for most of us, our big mouths don't usually get us in this much trouble! *(Both boys grin weakly.)*

Shaun: Dan, I'm really sorry. I don't know what else to say. I'll talk to Principal Graham in the morning—and anyone else you say.

Dan: Naw. He'll do. To tell you the truth—*(he stops and both boys laugh)* frankly, I'm sick of the whole mess. I just wish it could be over.

Shaun: Yeah, I know what you mean.

Dan: Listen, whaddaya say we get back to the youth group?

Shaun: OK, Dan. *(They start off together.)* Hey, Dan?

Dan: Yeah?

Shaun: Thanks, man!

Dan: No problem. *(Both boys laugh.)*

END OF SCENE 2

ACT 3 SCENE 3

Same auditorium as act one. Principal Graham is at the microphone. Danny and his family are on the platform behind him. Every member of the cast, plus extras are in the audience.

Graham: Students, parents, distinguished guests: As you know, I announced this special assembly on Monday, to give the parents and special guests time to arrange to be here. And, as you also know, we were gathered in this same auditorium just one week ago today to present a very special award to one of Oaklawn High's students. *(Pauses.)* You're all aware of what has taken place since then. *(Another pause.)* I want today's ceremony to be a festive occasion, so I'm *not* going to drag out the details and reprimand everyone involved. I'd probably miss someone anyway! *(Light laughter from the crowd.)* We all can take a lesson from this—the entire issue of whether or not Dan Mulligan cheated on his science project boils down to mindless, foundless, and wholly untrue *gossip!* *(Shouts and pounds the podium with each word. At his final word, the crowd cheers, stamps feet, claps, and rises to a standing ovation. Principal Graham turns and motions to Danny, who stands, grinning, joins Graham, and takes a bow.)* I had a great deal more to say, but after that response from you, it would be anticlimactic! *(Crowd laughs.)* Let me just say that the state review board did a careful examination of *every* applicant before the award was ever announced, and we should have trusted them. *(Grows very serious.)* But a thoughtless remark was dropped like a careless match, and the flame was fanned and fed with suppositions, innuendos, and more malicious remarks, until the fire burned out of control and nearly destroyed a young man's life! *(Crowd is hushed. Graham turns toward Mulligan family and lightens his tone and attitude.)* I know I said I wasn't going to preach, but I just couldn't resist that beautiful metaphor! *(Crowd breaks out laughing. Everyone is in a good mood now.)* Just let me close by saying that Danny and his father have been completely vindicated of all charges, and we, the school board, city government, and friends of the Mulligan family, sincerely hope that these unhappy events will quickly fade to a dim shadow of this bright and shining hour. *(Applause.)* Danny, allow me to once again present you with the first-place award for state champion in the 198_ National Junior Scientist of America competition.

(Crowd rises to its feet in cheers and applause as Danny comes forward to receive the award. He shakes hands with Graham, bows to the crowd, and the curtain falls.)

CURTAIN

Questions for Discussion

1. Danny's best friend, Shaun, was the first person to suggest that Danny had not earned the award. Did he actually say that Danny had cheated? What emotions might have prompted Shaun to say what he did? What happened to the rather vague accusation once Maria Thompson got ahold of it? What (misguided) emotions (concerning her father) influenced what Marie said?

2. Rumors grow along a gossip trail like a snowball rolling downhill. How is that illustrated in this play? How did each person add to the story and change it from groundless gossip to "fact"?

3. Rick, Rita, Fred, and Mr. Holt didn't believe the rumor and tried to stop it. Which of them was most successful? Why? The fact that none of them were able to stop the rumor points out how very dangerous a careless word can be—just like a match dropped in a dry forest. What warning does this give you about your own speech habits? What truth does this illustrate about the life-span of rumors?

4. When Mrs. Thompson heard that Danny had been officially accused of cheating, she said, "Why, who would say such a thing?" Why were Mr. and Mrs. Thompson worried?

What part had they played in the whole mess? Who had Mrs. Thompson been talking to? Were the things said about Mr. Mulligan true? What does this tell you about "blowing off steam" to people you are not really close to? What about repeating things to your friends that have been discussed at home? Even in the privacy of your home, is there ever really a time for telling lies about others?

5. The next day in school, Shaun told Dan that "other people" were saying these things, but that he had stuck up for Dan. Was this true? What do you think Shaun was trying to do? How did he probably feel at that time?

6. How do you feel about what Alicia said about being afraid to stick up for Danny? Was it because she wasn't sure about his guilt, or because she was afraid to go against the rest of the crowd?

7. Can you think of any reasons besides the ones named by the youth group (envy, jealousy, lack of love, peer pressure) why people gossip? Do you think people who respect themselves generally participate in gossip? Why or why not?

8. Jesus said (in Matthew 5:44), "Love your enemies and pray for those who persecute you, that you may be sons of your Father in heaven." How does this relate to gossip? Can you imagine Jesus gossiping? What is one really good way (the opposite of gossip) to love those who persecute you?